The Golden Age of Show Jumping

Frank Waters

The Golden Age Of Show Jumping

Frank Waters

Published by Sage Words Publishing www.sagewordspublishing.com

Author: Frank Waters

Editor: Jake George

ISBN-13: 978-0991501472

ISBN-10: 0991501470

Cover credit: Cover designed by author Frank Waters

Interior Photos:
Photos provided by the author, Frank Waters' with full rights to publish them in this book.

The Golden Age Of Show Jumping

Frank Waters

Contents

Dedicated to May Charles

Who was a great influence on my life since I was a teenager until she died in October 1980.

Foreword by Harvey Smith

The past year has been an incredible year for me; I helped my wife Sue train the Grand National winner, Auroras Encore, becoming one of only three ladies to do so and now Frank has asked me to write the foreword to his book with my good friend and team mate Paddy McMahon.

There is no one who knows more about the golden age of show jumping than Frank and I know he will have done us all proud – and told many stories about the mischief we got up to during those great days. I know how special this book is to Frank and to be part of this journey with him is a great honor. Through the years I've known Frank I've been very proud of everything he has achieved. Like me Frank fought his way to where he is today and no one deserves this success more than him.

I've known Frank since 1959 when he was an 11-year-old boy helping Southport rider Harry Priestley. I was riding Farmers Boy the brilliant horse who set me on the road to international success. When I had my first big international string of horses, O'Malley, Warpaint, Sea Hawk and Harvester, Frank helped my then groom Doreen, (Blossom) as she was known with my horses at the Southport show in Lancashire.

Doreen was also looking after a horse called Deric who was owned and ridden by my close friend Sammy Morphet from Woolton in Liverpool. At the end of the Show, my mother and Sammy's mother both gave him a half a crown each. It was only recently I discovered Frank still treasures those coins which is incredible and touching as my mother was special to me.

It was a great loss to show jumping when Frank had to give up riding, due to developing an allergy, but with proper northern grit he turned to commentating – and became one of the best in the world. It must have been devastating for Frank to have to give up riding, but he dug in there and through sheer hard work became one of the best

2

commentators in the world. I said years ago that he was the best show jumping commentator in the country something I still stand by. The Halifax Courier wrote an article which begins. When Harvey Smith acknowledges you are the best show jumping commentator there is, you know you have made the grade."

Over the years Frank became known as 'the man with the golden voice'. He went on to commentate at the Horse of the Year Show with Dorian Williams and later was invited by Lt. Col. Frank Beale to announce at the Windsor Park Equestrian Club, something he did for five years until he left for the United States in early 1980's, a loss to us all.

Frank has the wonderful gift of making everyone feel comfortable, he'd sit in the commentary box with H.R.H. Prince Phillip who owned the club and was able to chat as easily to royalty as he was the most humble groom and rider.

Now Frank has turned his hand to writing. I know that anything Frank does, he does well, something which makes me proud to be associated with his book. Well done Frank, I am really proud of you.

Foreword by Paddy McMahon

I have been fortunate to know Frank for most of my life having first met him when he competed against us back in the late sixties. It was a sad loss to show jumping when he developed an allergy to horses and had to give up riding. However, a year later Frank found his vocation as a commentator, something he was wonderful at. He went on to become one of the best in England.

I will never forget the night Frank was in the commentary booth at Wembley with Dorian Williams on that special occasion when I beat Paul Schocke-Mohle of Germany to win the Victor Ludorum. You could have heard a pin drop when I started that round and as the excitement built toward the last row of fences, a difficult combination, Forgie knew that we were going to win this and as I came over the last jump and through the finish in 28.3 seconds, more than eighteen thousand people in the stands erupted. Dorian was in tears as he shouted in excitement. "She's done it, 28.3 oh, what a fantastic victory." Frank could not get a word in edgeways as all of the crowd were on their feet cheering.

Frank told me later that he could not have said much anyway because he also was so emotional. It was an absolutely amazing occasion.

It is moments like this in one's career that you can never ever forget. I will certainly never forget that night at Wembley. It was so wonderful that Frank was a part of that special night.

It was a great loss to British Show Jumping, when Frank moved to the United States. He is still missed in Show Jumping circles here in Britain.

Frank is a tremendously talented old school announcer but our loss was America's gain.

Now Frank has become an author and has written this amazing book, The Golden Age of Show Jumping. Who better to write about all of us from that wonderful time than Frank who was there with us? I could not be more proud to be writing the foreword for it along with my old rival Harvey Smith. I feel so honored to be part of this piece of history and I wish him all the luck with this book.

Good luck Frank and on behalf of all of the great riders and horses of that special time we thank you for bringing a magical time in our sport back to the living rooms of Great Britain.

Chapter One

I was about three years of age when I had my first experience with a horse. At that time, my parents lived with my grandparents and in those days, our milk was delivered by horse and cart. I remember Kitty well; she was a big bay mare with the gentlest nature you could wish in a horse. Every morning when I heard the rattle of milk bottles down School Lane, I would run out with potato and carrot peelings my mother had saved from the previous evening. Kitty was used to getting her treat, she always knew I would be there waiting for her and every time gave that gentle little neigh when she saw me.

I had no idea then that my love for her would take me into the fantasy world of International Show Jumping and to travel the world including announcing the Asian Games, Doha 2006 and the Pan Arab Games December 2011. All I knew was that the warmth of her breath and the velvety feel of her nuzzle was something that tugged at my heart and I totally fell in love with her.

My grandfather had a tremendous interest in Kitty also, somewhere on School Lane where we live, she always left him a large present which he proceeded to shovel up and put around his roses, he had the best roses around thanks to my four-legged friend.

‍ಣ

Seven days a week for as long as I can remember I greeted Kitty until one day while out on my bicycle, I passed a farm not far from home to discover this enormous grey Clydesdale grazing in a field, I had never seen anything so big, he stood about 18 hands 2 inches and at first, I was a little afraid. His color and size fascinated me and I rode by every day until one day, I took him some of the potato and carrot peelings. He was grazing at quite a distance from me and I was still afraid not knowing him, he looked nothing like Kitty and by now I was no more than four or five years old! I decided to call him over, not knowing his name I just yelled, hello to be totally ignored. I was disappointed of course, so left my gift of peelings on the ground the other side of the gate and proceeded to do this for a few days. I guess he found them, because each day that I rode over there to see him, they were gone.

I almost gave up on ever having this massive horse as a friend when one day the farmer came over to the field while I was there to catch the horse and called out his name, Billy. Billy looked up, let out a loud neigh and came galloping toward us at thundering speed. I was petrified, having never seen a horse run that fast before and his size virtually made the ground shake. I almost ran when the farmer told me not to be afraid, he said, "Billy wouldn't hurt a fly". He had this enormous leather contraption in his hand, which later I was to learn was called a head collar, or halter. Billy pushed his nose into it, the farmer buckled it up and then handed Billy a handful of sugar cubes.

And this is what made Billy gallop to the gate every time he brought him in; he knew that his treat was waiting.

I did not say a word. The farmer asked me if I would like to see where Billy lived. Obviously, he did not have to ask me twice, I pushed my bicycle into this big yard and there was this wonderful old stone stable block and Billy was led into the largest stable. I remember the sweet smell of straw that had been laid down for Billy and there was a big iron frame screwed on the wall full of hay. There was also a large tin bucket on the floor full of fresh water and an empty large container screwed to the wall. I was to learn later that this was where Billy's food was put for him to eat, in those days it was purely Bran and Oats. This was nothing like we feed horses today. No supplements; horse and pony cubes, linseed, barley, vitamins and horses still lived until they were thirty and more. There were different birds flying in and out, mostly swallows and I saw nests made of mud up in the rafters, these birds did not faze Billy at all and he seemed very content. I was in awe with this new world and even more so when the farmer started to put this enormous leather collar around Billy's neck followed by the bridle, blinkers, reins and a crup that was inserted under his tail. I did not realize at the time, but the farmer was getting Billy ready to go out and plough a field. I can see this as if it were yesterday, for a giant, he was so gentle and to this day, I remember the special bond Mr. Rimmer, the farmer had with Billy, they seemed to be best friends with great respect for each other.

I followed Mr. Rimmer and Billy out of the stable yard and out to a field at the back of his farm and watched in fascination as Mr. Rimmer hitched Billy to the plough, then off they went around the field, I can still hear the jingle from the chains that hitched him to the plough. This was a first for me and after it was all over I asked Mr. Rimmer why he had done this, he told me that he was preparing the field to plant potatoes.

That was the first time I realized potatoes grew in the ground, now remember, I was about four years old and knew nothing about farming. The biggest thrill was about to come, at the finish of ploughing the field, Mr. Rimmer unhitched Billy then asked me if I would like to ride him back to his stable. I had never sat on a horse before and I remember the excitement building inside me, however, I was also afraid, having never been on a real horse. I was shocked and quite speechless, before I knew it, Mr. Rimmer had placed me on Billy's back and the only thing I can remember is, I almost stopped breathing, it was such an experience. I can still smell that horsey smell only those involved know, I can see the long neck, his mane, ears and the enormous height I was from the ground, it felt like I was in the clouds, yet immediately formed this enormous bond with my new giant friend, Billy!

I was brought up in a strict English home including being taught great manners by my grandmother, however, I did not want to get off Billy's back. I did not argue of course but immediately asked Mr. Rimmer when I could sit on Billy's back again.

ଔ

He told me that more ploughing would be done in another field the following Saturday and I could ride Billy back to his stable once again. Of course, I hardly slept the whole week and could not wait for the following Saturday to arrive and saved every potato and carrot peeling in a bag for Billy.

Unfortunately for Kitty, the milk horse, she got half her rations every day while the rest was saved for my new friend, but of course, I rode Billy and this made him extremely special. My love for the horse was now born and firmly ensconced in my heart, though at that early age, I did not realize how much and that this chance meeting would eventually take me around the world both in the saddle and announcing some of the biggest events on the planet!

Being a grey, which I learned from Mr. Rimmer, because I thought Billy was white, he showed much more dirt than darker horses so I would watch him being washed and groomed with total fascination. How I longed to do it, however, at the age of four, I could not reach much higher than Billy's knees, but I was allowed to brush his legs. I had no idea in those days that horses could kick, but not Billy, he was so gentle and absolutely took care of me when I was in his stable. I knew that he would never hurt me and I gave my full trust to this gentle giant, I adored this horse and started telling friends that he was mine, in my heart this is what I believed! It must have been two years that I rode my bicycle to see Billy every single day.

ଓ

One day, I rode down to see him and Billy was not in the field, I cycled over to his stable, no Billy. Mr. Rimmer must have seen me from the window and came out, I had never seen a grown man cry before and he was crying. Billy had developed very bad colic in the night and had to be put down.

I did not understand death at that time, however, I knew it was bad and also started to cry, I can remember Mr. Rimmer rocking me and telling me that everything was going to be alright. It was not of course, because neither he nor I would ever see our gentle giant again. The wonderful, kind and big hearted Billy that gave me so much love for the horse; which one day would become such a part of my life, had gone forever.

Chapter Two

It is amazing how fate plays such a part in our lives, it took a while to get over the death of Billy, I think being so young and never experiencing death before, it left quite a scar. When Billy died, I was six and going to a convent school not far from home and I did not know its association with horses, I was about to find out.

During the summer, they had a garden fete and I constantly begged Reverend Mother for something to do, I just wanted to help. Unbeknown to me, there was a lady who had arrived with two ponies to give rides with the proceeds going to the convent.

It turned out she was a former pupil of St. Anne's and was called Mary, Mary Bowler. Her father Tom had started Bowlers riding school years before and I was about to become part of this establishment. Little did I know that one day I would have a full time job with Mary and that we would become lifelong friends?

Reverend Mother told me to go and help Mary give the rides, I was so excited, this could not have been a better job for me. Of course, Mary was quite enthralled with me and introduced me to Johnny and Toby. Johnny was a 13:2 hh. Piebald, a paint pony as they call it in the United States and Toby was a Shetland full of mischief and was known as a scoundrel.

❧

Mary kept charge of Toby, he was to give rides to the very small children, she handed me the lead rein for Johnny and he was the one I led up and down and gave the bigger children and some adults pony rides. I was only six years old and felt very important and all afternoon collected sixpence per ride from each of the children or their parents. I felt sad at the end of the day when Mary left. However, she did not leave without me getting all the information from her as to the riding school address and how to get there! This was on Saturday and Monday evening after school I was riding my bicycle furiously down Brewery Lane on the way to the stables. As I rode down the dirt track at the side of Mary and her parent's house, I started to get that wonderful smell that only horse lovers appreciate and suddenly there it was in full view. There were about four rows of stables, a large barn full of hay and straw, a tack room, rider's lounge, a muckheap and some arenas where lessons were taught. At that time, there were no indoor arenas.

I walked into the tack room after parking my bicycle and saw some girls older than me cleaning tack. There must have been fifty saddles and bridles, loose bits, stirrup irons and other wonderful treasures hanging on nails, horseshoes nailed on the walls and quite a few halters.

CR

This was a new experience for me and the smell of saddle soap as they cleaned was heaven. I can still smell that tack room as if it were yesterday and I so wanted to join in. I was a little embarrassed owing to the fact that I was being stared at; these girls did not know me and asked who I was? I told them about helping Mary the previous Saturday at the Garden Fete and to my disappointment, they did not seem in the least impressed. Mary had not mentioned me to anybody and I felt kind of awkward, did I have a right to be here, I was soon to find out?

It was summer time in England and it does not get dark until well after ten so Mary was out on a ride.

Many riders paid six shillings (about 75 cents) an hour to go out riding and off they would go on the country lanes, sometimes as many as fifteen to twenty at a time. The country lanes then were beautiful, full of trees, blossoms and many varieties of wild grasses with little traffic. I have such vivid memories of the beauty of the English countryside in those days, few houses and hardly any cars on the roads. Eventually, I would be a part of this; however, at that time I just wanted to be accepted as a member of this select group of people who like me, loved horses.

CR

There was a bench outside the tack room and I walked outside and sat down, it was about fifteen minutes later I heard the ride coming home and I could not believe how many ponies and horses there were. Leading them of course was Mary on her favorite pony, Whiskey; I found out later, only Mary rode him, her special pony.

I was also to find out that Whiskey had a bit of a temper and could give a nasty bite, so we had to be careful being around him. Only Mary and one of the grooms handled him, he had little trust with people.

Nobody gave me any attention and I stayed pretty quiet sitting there alone on the bench. The girls who were cleaning the tack came out and started to take the ponies away as the riders dismounted. Some were put in their individual stalls while others got turned out into the grazing field where they lived and were given hay. The ones that were going on the next ride remained tacked up and the next set of riders mounted and walked around the yard until Mary was ready to go. I took it all in and did not miss a beat, this is what I wanted and I wanted to know it all. I was desperate for Mary to look over and acknowledge me; it didn't happen, as she was far too busy to notice me. After the ride had left, I rode home on my bicycle feeling slightly sad.

However, I knew it would not be long before I was back in the stable yard at Bowlers Riding School.

❧

On the following Saturday, back I rode on my bicycle and found some of the same girls cleaning tack and there were others I had not seen before. A couple remarked that I was back including this very horsey looking girl called Jennifer who a few weeks later became one of my friends. She asked me if I had ever taken a bridle apart and cleaned it. Of course I hadn't but I told her I had so she gave me one and asked me to do just that. Taking it apart was easy, all one did was undo the buckles and dismantle it. Now there were quite a few pieces, the headpiece, brow band, cheek pieces, nose band, bit and reins. I soaked the bit in a bucket of water as I had watched the girls do, cleaned every piece of leather and left a little too much saddle soap on. That was not the problem the main problem was putting it back together again exactly as it had been before Jennifer handed it to me.

She saw that I was unsure of this and decided to help, thank God. In my mind, I actually believed that Mary would kill me because I had ruined one of her bridles. Of course, Mary still did not know I was even there as she was in the schooling ring as we called it giving a lesson.

When she eventually finished, she actually came into the tack room to look at the book that had all the rider's names in it to see who was coming that weekend for lessons or rides. She saw me and smiled and I remember her very words "Oh, you found us then, I see the girls have put you to work already?"

ભ

I was delighted that she recognized me. Nevertheless, I was rather embarrassed in front of everyone that Mary Bowler had acknowledged me. I guess being completely new to all of this, I really felt out of my depth. Remember, with Billy, all I ever did was ride him back to the barn led by Mr. Rimmer, I had never been taught how to take care of tack, a horse and the everyday running of a riding establishment.

Mary then turned leaving me with the girls and went about her business with the riders who were outside waiting to mount the ponies for the next ride. It took no time for me to learn how to take apart a bridle quickly, clean it and put it back together again. Then Jennifer showed me how to do the same with a saddle, taking off the stirrups, leathers and girth. After cleaning it underneath, the flaps, seat and all the parts, I then put it back together and onto the wooden saddle horse where it lived.

I did this for about a month and absolutely loved it and eventually Jennifer showed me how to sweep the stable yard. It was cobbled and always looked beautiful until the ponies and horses put their heads over the door and dropped loads of hay as they ate. This is when the brushes came out again and we all swept away to make it pristine once again.

ભ

The amazing thing in those days was the number of youngsters who were willing to work and work for no pay because they loved this little world of horses so much.

It was a little while before Jennifer showed me how to muck out the stalls and that was an enormous thrill.

I really felt like I had finally arrived the first time Jennifer put a pitchfork in my hand, I felt so important and was now accepted as part of the group. Mary did not pay a lot of attention to us, she was far too busy, however, she just seemed to accept that we loved what we did and left us to it. I did notice that some of the girls rode at least once a week; however, I would never be as bold as to ask when I was going to ride.

This was to happen soon enough though, I didn't realize that Mary had taken notice as to how hard I was trying and willing to work any way I could by cleaning tack, sweeping the yard, mucking out stalls, brushing off ponies, filling water buckets, filling hay nets and even bringing the horses in from the fields when it came to lesson time. She knew that my favorite was Johnny; he was so gentle, kind and would not hurt a fly.

I fully trusted him and he was one of the most loved of all Mary's ponies.

ভ

Even talking to the odd person I keep in touch with they still remember some of the names. There was Johnny, of course, Toby, Whiskey, Blaze, (who had one eye) Pinnie, Monty and many others. Now at this time, I had never ridden before without someone leading me, in fact, the only horse I had ever ridden was Billy. I had watched quite a few lessons by now and had an idea how to sit and how to hold the reins. Boy was I in for a shock? I had only ever been led back to the stables on Billy and that was bareback holding on to his mane. It is a totally different experience having to sit on a saddle, hold reins, use your legs and steer a horse. The most important lesson was to keep those toes up and heels down, I could not remember at first which way was which!

The time had arrived and Mary promised me that at the end of the day, I could have fifteen minutes riding Johnny. I could hardly contain myself with excitement. When the time arrived, I was told how to put my foot in the stirrup, swing around, grab the cantle of the saddle and pull myself on, this was the easy part. I sat there in the saddle and was actually afraid, scared I was going to make a complete fool of myself and fall off. I did not fall off, however, I did not have a clue how to position my feet in the irons or how to position myself in the saddle.

ভ

I clumsily grabbed the reins and immediately felt that this was the most embarrassing moment of my life. I believed every person in that riding school was looking at me, never giving it a thought that they had all been there at one time or another. Mary was sympathetic and told me to relax while she positioned my feet with the toes up and the heels down. She then asked me to push myself comfortably into the saddle telling me if I wanted to, I could hold on to Johnny's mane. Off we went around the yard and after about five minutes I started to relax, I was riding a horse, fully tacked and holding on to the reins.

I did not care how many eyes watched me and I knew that one day I would be a good rider, little did I know that I would be jumping five foot fences and competing in horse shows by the time I was a teenager. However, at that moment in time, I wanted it to last forever.

I continued my every spare moment at Mary Bowlers riding school and got better as time went by including jumping over a pole supported by two small oilcans. I remember the first time Johnny jumped it with me and his neck hit me in the face. I had no idea how to go forward with a horse, but this got better with time also, I learned a lot from Johnny, and of course, Mary. Like everyone, we kept her yard working every day and in those days, nobody got paid except the full time staff.

ଔଃ

I believe they only earned about three pounds a week, (Six Dollars) working six and a half days at a time, twelve hours a day. Mary employed two grooms and they ran everything, including the booking of all the lessons and rides.

Mary was the teacher and of course, the owner of this very prestigious establishment, it is still there to this day and one of the most sought after riding schools in the county of Lancashire. I also hear that Mary is still sort of running things, even in her eighties, however, she must have an unbelievable staff today and everything is running like clockwork.

Not far away, there was another riding school owned and operated by a Mrs. Walsh, she had a head girl by the name of Hilary who eventually became a friend of mine, but it took a very big second from Mary's establishment.

I spent about four years at Bowlers riding school and often heard Mary talk about a family that had ridden there as children from Ainsdale, about three miles away. This family had now grown and travelled the show jumping circuit with a couple of horses. Mary was very proud of them, especially being her former pupils who started off riding with her as children.

ଔଃ

This family was known as the Priestley's with Harry and Doreen Priestley being the two siblings who travelled the show jumping circuit. There were other siblings however, only Harry and Doreen were involved with horse shows and it became a mission of mine to travel with them. I thought it would be incredible to see another side of the equestrian world I knew nothing about so I got on my bicycle one day

16

and rode down to the farm where the Priestley's kept their horses. On arrival at the farm, there was this elegant Rover car in the driveway and an older man was talking to this beautiful big bay Irish Hunter over the fence of a field, the horse was called Tommy. He was actually giving Tommy cigarettes that the horse proceeded to eat. I watched this from a little distance when suddenly, Mr. Priestley asked who I was and if he could help me. I told him that I wanted to take care of the horses and he smiled, I was eleven years old, maybe twelve.

He thought it kind of amusing that such a young boy wanted to take care of horses this big and strong. Little did he know that Tommy and I would become a perfect match with unbelievable trust and love for one another? Mr. Priestley told me the address of their house and asked me to come and meet his daughter Doreen and son Harry. I believe I kept up with his car down Liverpool Road until I arrived at their house never having pedaled my bicycle so fast in my life. On arrival, I saw this big detached home and I don't believe until then I had ever been in a house this big, nor as beautiful.

∞

Doreen was the sweetest lady and I remember. She was doing the laundry; she was very amused like her father that such a young, small boy wanted to take care of these big horses. They had another horse called Star they had just bought him as a five-year-old, a black thoroughbred who was as skitty as they come and had just arrived about two weeks before from a dealer in Scotland.

Doreen was concerned that I might get hurt, but I was not afraid and assured them after meeting Harry, a character that I could handle it. They took a chance and I became their groom at the age of eleven, or was it twelve? My life in Show Jumping had begun and I had no idea what was in store, that day in 1960 which changed my life to what it has become today. Now the adventure begins when Tommy was brought in from the field after wintering out and the first priority was to clean him up and get him fit for the shows. I was told by Doreen that his show name was Caruso, this under the rules of the B.S.J.A. is what he jumped under and he had a bit of an attitude. I learned that day having never heard of it before what the B.S.J.A. was, the British Show Jumping Association, the governing body of Show Jumping in Britain, I could not wait to become a member.

∞

This was early March and it was still cold in England so the task at hand was not easy with ice still on the roads on some days. In England, we always got the horses fit with a tremendous amount of roadwork; however, at this time I had only ridden riding school ponies. I had gained quite a bit of riding experience but this was a totally different kettle of fish, I was about to ride a 16:2 hh show jumper, big, strong not to mention that he had not been ridden for 6 months. I had spent a few days getting to know Tommy and Star, feeding, watering, mucking out, grooming and I think my time around them had built trust and respect. I had fallen for Tommy, Harry was the only one to ride Star and occasionally Doreen, but I did most of the riding on Tommy. The first time was a challenge however; Harry rode out with me on Star, this happened most of the time at the beginning until he felt I was capable of riding him alone. Boy, was I proud when that day arrived and I wanted to ride over to everyone I knew to show them that I could ride a Show Jumper. First stop was at Mary Bowlers to show them all my new steed, there was a little jealousy as no one could believe that I had brought the sheen out on Tommy's coat the way I had. I spent hours grooming him and now that his winter coat had fully gone, he looked amazing, getting fitter by the day.

ೞ

About two miles from where the horses stabled, Harry had a paddock full of show jumps and we started riding over there about three times a week as he jumped and schooled the horses. After a couple of weeks of this Harry told me that the following Saturday, we would be going to our first show. I was so excited and started getting the horsebox ready for this trip, scrubbing it and laying down straw for the horses to be comfortable on their travels. I had no idea what famous Show Jumpers would be at this show if any and what new adventures awaited?

My show jumping life was about to begin as I entered this new world of horses and riders full of celebrities and new friends.

Chapter Three

I remember well the Thursday, two days before I was to set off on my first trip with Harry and Doreen. It was to be a one-day show in Cheshire and in those days in England, we always had wonderful long summer days, even though this was late spring. I was listening to a transistor radio that my grandmother had bought me and the weather forecast came on telling us that Saturday had a possibility of strong thunderstorms. I could not believe this as we had not experienced any bad weather so far this year and I felt quite deflated believing that we would not go to the show. Thursday was a lovely day and I rode Tommy that evening on the beautiful country road that winded for several miles outside of our stable yard.

The trees were in full bloom and I will always remember the fragrances of Formby old road as it twisted and turned with nothing but fields either side, all changed now. The most beautiful part of this was the amazing old oak trees that grew on both sides of the road, one after the other meeting in the middle. This formed the most beautiful arch of branches and leaves with rays of sun constantly shining through.

ᙍ

I was always in awe by this, and all that existed in this glorious tunnel of nature was Tommy and myself. The two of us just plodded along with not a care in the world and he rarely spooked at anything. We had such trust in each other by this time and had really formed a bond. He was a wonderful horse and was more than used to being out on the road. Of course, in those days, we had very little traffic and with the traffic we had, drivers were always courteous when they saw a horse coming and slowed way down, some even stopping completely. In the back of my mind, I was focusing on Saturday, two days away and praying that we would not get the predicted thunderstorm. Tommy and I walked and trotted for at least an hour and a half down these beautiful country roads and I knew that this was constantly building muscle on Tommy, nothing better than long trots on a solid road for fitness. On our arrival back at the stable, Harry was there to ride out on Star and he always referred to Tommy as Tommy Horse. He always teased him and that often made Tommy a little mad, laying back his ears and shaking his head. After Harry left on Star, I washed Tommy off with a soapy sponge, rinsed him and then dried him off before putting him back in his stable.

ଔ

I often spent hours in there just talking with him while I lay on his straw and he was nothing but gentle and always seemed to listen. He definitely became my best friend and he was the world to me and he triggered my imagination many times about him and I riding in the Olympics.

I never rode him in competition though as he was Harry's best horse and was often in the award ceremonies. After I had bedded him down I got Star's stable ready for him coming back with Harry, I filled the water buckets, then prepared their hay nets and feed for the night. Eventually, I could hear the clip clop of Star coming back down the road and soon saw them turning into the stable yard. Harry took off his saddle and we washed out the sweat mark underneath, groomed him and put him away in his stable.

Harry then told me that he would only be taking Tommy to the show on Saturday as Star was not quite ready and wanted to take it slowly with him. I did not mention the thunderstorm and bad weather that was forecasted, however, it was very much on my mind that we would not be going to the show.

After feeding the horses and making sure they were settled for the night, I said goodnight to Harry, got on my bicycle and rode home. My parent's house was at least six miles from the stables and I rode this journey every day for about three years, even in the winter, more about that later in the story.

ଔ

The next day was Friday; a beautiful blue sky with sunshine and I was feeling hopeful about Saturday, however, one can never predict the weather, especially in England. I did my paper route in the early morning as I always did, came home, had breakfast and rode off to school on my bicycle. It was not an easy day because of my excitement about the show tomorrow. I do remember Mrs. Kenny, my English teacher telling us to write an essay on our favorite subject. I of course, wrote all about my dream of becoming an Olympic rider, it just seemed to flow and in my mind I was there competing and representing Great Britain. In my young mind, the Olympic Games were local and everyone I knew came out to see me. Of course, I won the Gold Medal and the crowd went crazy, as I was the only one from all teams that jumped a double clear round.

Mrs. Kenny was quite impressed and asked me to read my essay to the class. Some were a little jealous of my involvement with horses and tittered in a mocking way, I didn't care, to me; I just felt that they would never do what I was doing. Amazing really, as I had still not gone to my first show, that was to be the very next day and I told the class this with glee. Many of them did not believe me, and thought I was living in this fantasyland, however, I knew the truth. I left school that evening and could not peddle fast enough down to the stables to prepare for the following day.

ଓ

On the way, I noticed a buildup of clouds from the west and was feeling mad at the weather. On my arrival, I tacked up Tommy who by now gave a wonderful deep neigh every time he heard me coming. We set off on a shortened ride that evening, as I wanted him to be fresh for the show the next day, if we were going that is? I just did a little walking and trotting with him and hardly built a sweat.

I gave him an extra grooming, washed his feet and I remember putting on a tail bandage hoping his tail would look wonderful the next day. I was closely watching the sky which was getting darker and really irritating me. I got some hot water, a large block of glycerin saddle soap and proceeded to clean all of Tommy's tack, saddle, leathers, irons, brushing boots and of course, his bridle. I wanted him to look the best and prettiest horse at the show, if we went that is. I then put the tack into the horsebox with a grooming kit and everything we would need for the journey including two buckets and a full net of hay. After everything was completed, I left for the night and started to cycle home only to feel rain on my face half way on my journey. Still no sound of thunder, yet, I knew it was on its way because the weatherman had said so on the radio.

Ↄ

This being my first show, I wanted to look the part so I laid out my white riding breeches, polished top boots, shirt, tie and jacket.

I knew that it was not me who was riding in the show, however, I didn't care, I wanted everyone to believe I was the rider. During the night I heard the thunder and rain, heavy rain, lots of lightening and big bangs. I was not sleeping anyway, far too excited and never gave it a thought that we would not be going to Cheshire. At five thirty a.m. I was up, dressed and ready to go. Nobody in their right mind was up at that hour in my parent's house and I crept out of the back door, grabbed my bicycle out of the shed, put on a large plastic cape and set off in the rain. It was still dark and the thunder had stopped, but still raining. As luck would have it, the storm had arrived earlier than expected and the thunder had already passed through to the east of us. As I rode the six miles to the farm in Woodvale, I noticed the rain was getting a little less and I was feeling hopeful. Tommy always knew when I was close; he always gave that little neigh to let me know that he knew I was arriving.

Of course, he also knew that he would be getting breakfast pretty soon and Star was also learning that breakfast was close by.

Ↄ

Star was also a part of my life in Woodvale, however, I never rode him and Harry had much more to do with him than I did, he was Harry's baby and he totally left Tommy to me, except at the shows of course.

The sun rises early in England during the late spring and summer and it was peeking over the horizon as I arrived giving me a glance at the sky. I was hopeful as there were tons of blue and the cloud was definitely breaking up. The rain was coming and going in small light showers and something told me that we would definitely be going to Cheshire. By now, it was just after 6 a.m. I fed the horses and started to groom Tommy while he was still eating. It never fazed him while I was doing this, yet if Harry came near him while he was eating he would lay his ears back, shake his head and show him the whites of his eyes.

Harry always teased Tommy this way, as he was really a big kid at heart; he was probably in his early twenties then. I knew that we would be leaving about 9 a.m., and still had plenty of time to make sure everything was ready for the journey. At about half past eight, Harry arrived with his sister Doreen who proceeded to take all kinds of bags and boxes out of the car and asked me to assist her in getting everything into the horsebox.

ରଃ

Now I really knew it was happening, we were on the way to our first horse show together and the weather was getting better by the minute. The horsebox was kind of unique with a large cab and two stalls that were partitioned behind the cab. The middle of the horsebox was living quarters with a built in sofa that became a bed. There was a sink, a stove and lots of built in cupboards, and it also had its own private door. The back of the horsebox was another single stall for one more horse.

From the living area, there was a door into each of the horse's stalls so that we could go back and forth if we travelled in the living area. I could not believe the wonderful treats that Doreen had made for us including sandwiches, homemade cakes, chocolates, different cheeses, crackers, bread and cans of soup. In the boxes she had packed pots, pans, teapots, cups, plates, cutlery and everything needed for a fully-fledged dinner. I did not realize at the time, but all of these items were to stay in the horsebox in different draws and cupboards for the season. Once all of this was done, Doreen took charge and we let down the ramp so that we could load Tommy for the journey to the show.

ରଃ

This is when I found out we were all going to Cheadle Hulme, a pretty village in the heart of Cheshire that was holding a one-day horse show. Tommy looked absolutely a star as I led him from his stable to the horsebox with his leg wraps, tail bandage and shiny leather halter.

I felt so proud and grown up as he just followed me up the ramp and Harry showed me how to tie the rope through the big ring on the wall. I will always remember as we closed and locked the ramp Star neighing out loud and Tommy answering him, I always felt that Star wanted to go with us that day.

Harry got into the driver's side and I guided him back as he reversed this enormous horsebox out of its parking spot where it had spent the winter. Doreen and I climbed into the cab and we were on our way, words cannot describe my excitement as we drove out of the yard on the first of many, many adventures together to horse shows around the region.

Chapter Four

The first thing we had to do was stop at a local petrol station and fill up as the horsebox had not been out of the yard since September and it was now April the following year.

I remember how proud I felt, as in England in those days everyone stared at horseboxes always believing that some famous rider or horses were on board. To me, Tommy was the most famous horse of all and I wanted everyone to know him, he was the most special animal alive and I wanted to shout it to the world. We filled up with petrol and set off on our journey to a world I had never known or seen before. I had been to the local Formby Show, however, I had never seen it from the other side, that of the horse and rider who had come to entertain the locals. They always turned out in force to support their one-day show that came around once a year.

I remember Harry driving the horsebox down the East Lancashire Road toward Manchester, one of the busiest roads in England at the time; it was exciting and mysterious as I had never been in a horsebox before. I saw people looking at us from cars and waving, of course, I waved back.

Most people in England always seemed to be fascinated by a horsebox. I don't even know if Great Britain had motorways in those days, in fact, I am sure there was none. I do remember talk of one being built which is now the M1, probably the busiest in England.

Ë

By this time, the sun was shining bright as ever and I just knew that it was going to be a perfect day in every way. After more than an hour driving, we entered the beautiful countryside of Cheshire. Perfect country lanes, vivid green trees, fields of mustard growing and, of course, many different types of animals grazing lazily, including horses. This was my first trip to the county of Cheshire and I noticed some wonderful old Tudor buildings with their black and white beams glowing in the sunshine. It had lots of history, halls, farms, big country houses and of course Tudor villages that we drove through on our way to Cheadle Hulme. I took it all in not wanting to miss one bit of this most exciting day of my life.

Suddenly ahead of us, I saw another horsebox and could hardly contain myself, as I knew we were getting close to the show ground. I had no idea who this horsebox belonged to but I heard Harry say to Doreen, 'looks like Judy is here'. I was to meet Judy later on that day and neither of us knew how she would one day many years from now play a big part in my immigration to the United States. Tommy sensed we were getting close to the show ground and neighed in the back quite loudly, he had been to many shows and this was nothing new to him but he sensed what was happening.

છ

Suddenly I saw the big tents ahead of us, the flags and I could see the arena in the middle of it all. Talk about hardly containing myself as I also saw about three rows of horseboxes lined up by the fence. My heart raced and my brain was in overdrive wondering which of our famous riders was going to be with us that day.

As we pulled in, Harry parked next to the horsebox we had followed and I saw this pretty lady getting out of the passenger side and an older gentleman getting out of the driver's door. It turned out to be Judy and she waved shouting hello to Harry and Doreen. Her father was the one driving and I remember a mop of grey hair and the rather nice sheepskin jacket he was wearing. It turned out that they were Jack and Judith Ollerton from Bolton in Lancashire. He owned a car dealership and Judy had a full time life with her horses. She brought three with her and I was to learn their names as Little Doris, Lady Nella and Diplomat. After Harry introduced me to her and Mr. Ollerton, I was starting to feel that I had arrived on the Show Jumping circuit. The first thing we did was lower the ramp and bring Tommy down, tying him up outside the horsebox. He was a little excited and sweating from the journey. I remember filling a bowl with some cold water and sponging him down while I gave him a net full of hay. He settled quickly and took everything in his stride; it was going to be at least another two hours before the class he was to ride in.

છ

Doreen and I walked to the secretary's tent to pick up Harry's number having been entered via mail several weeks before. There was a man in there that spoke to Doreen and I remember her laughing with him and called him Curly. I was to get to know him as a great character; he was the collecting ring steward at many shows throughout England. His name was Curly Beard, brother of Donald who at that time held the high jump record in Great Britain, and father of Carol who rode a super horse called Mayfly that she had won the leading show jumper of the year on at Wembley. I remember her groom, Wendy, who I was introduced to by Doreen which made me feel like a star - I had met the groom of the leading show jumper of the year! I still had not met Carol, however, that was to happen a few weeks later, even though I saw her ride at Cheadle Hulme.

Wendy was a character and I never knew on that day how one day in the future we would end up working together.

After we had picked up the number for Harry's classes, we walked around the show ground and saw many things including the tent full of children's pets that had all been judged. There was a tent full of wonderful home baking including biscuits, pies, cakes and other gourmet goodies that looked delicious. A tent full of many different types of vegetables, some were enormous and all had ribbons stuck on them having been judged early that morning.

ಚ

Next came Doreen's favorite, the 'Flower' tent, she loved flowers eventually becoming a flower arranger having gone to night school to learn this craft. After our little jaunt together around the show ground, we headed back to the horsebox and I was amazed how many of the riders waved and shouted hello to Doreen. I wondered if I would get to meet them also, I had nothing to worry about, it would happen soon enough. I remember one particular guy from Blackpool by the name of Johnny Greenwood who was quite friendly and had a couple of nice horses and it appeared he and Doreen had known each other from childhood. They had ridden against each other in the Pony classes and though Doreen was not competing anymore, they still remained great friends. Johnny was a very friendly guy and would eventually ride on the British Team and win major classes at the Horse of the Year Show and many other major shows in Great Britain. He came from an area that was known for its Equestrians and within a thirty-five-mile radius of

Johnny's home, many good riders had come from that neck of the woods, even Blackpool and Lytham St. Annes.

Pretty soon it was close to the class that Harry was to ride Tommy in, so I tacked him up and got him ready for competition. Once he was tacked, I gave him a final brush and after giving Harry a leg up, we headed for the collecting ring to warm him up.

ଔ

I noticed that many of the young horses were excited, some attending their very first show. Tommy was an old hand at this and was a perfect gentleman. On arrival, Harry greeted a lady on a magnificent horse, I remember him saying "Hello Valma" and they rode around together for a little while before Harry cantered off to get Tommy ready for his practice jumps. I learned later as she rode in the ring that her name was Valma Craig. Again, little did I know that fate would put me in her employ several years later after she had married her husband, Peter Milner.

Soon Harry was ready to take some practice jumps with Tommy so Doreen and I proceeded to put up a vertical of two poles. I had to concentrate really hard as many riders were out there and I did not want to miss the famous ones who came to compete that day. Tommy seemed to be jumping well and we moved over to the big spread fence and schooled Tommy over that.

He was about tenth to go in the class of about fifty riders; they were big classes in those days. When the time came for Tommy to enter the ring, I had no idea how nervous I would be as he started his round. The judges rang the bell and off he cantered around the ring. From what I remember, we had no timers in those days and everything was done with a stopwatch. This was the first round and from what I recall it was two rounds followed by one against the clock.

ଔ

Doreen was far more nervous than I and completely on edge the whole time Harry was in the arena. He was two fences from home and was clear, he jumped the next from last and headed for the last fence, as he took off, Doreen grabbed my arm and as Tommy landed the crowd started to applaud his clear round. I could not have been more excited, especially as Doreen was jumping up and down and hugging me like crazy.

Harry came out of the ring with an enormous smile on his face and with many horses still to go in the first round, we had no choice but to take Tommy back to the horsebox and tie him up. Obviously with him having to go again, I had to take his hay net away, it would not be good for him to eat and then go and compete. I did however give him a little bran and oats as it would be at least a couple of hours before his next round and covered him in a sweat blanket. He was the second to go clear and we had many horses and riders yet to compete. We walked down to the ring to watch some of the class and other riders started to arrive. There was Curly at the gate doing an amazing job keeping things moving and as always, making everyone laugh. I then remember a lady arriving on this beautiful horse called Nicki, her name was Jean Goodwin, eventually to become Mrs. Stephen Davenport. Stephen was a National Hunt jockey and had ridden in the Grand National, one of the, if not the most prestigious horse race in the world.

Jean had another horse called Hobo and I was fascinated with her and these two horses. Jean always travelled with her sister Pat and I was to learn, she was one of Britain's most successful show jumping riders. More about Jean at a later date though she entered the ring and immediately rode a beautiful clear round on Nicki. She was also a Cheshire resident, born and raised here and I believe, still lives there today. The class continued and from what I remember, there were about twelve or thirteen clear rounds. They jumped over a slightly shortened course, though not against the clock, unless of course, we had no clear round then they would have to go again. Rules were very different in those days, though I have to say, competition flowed and we never had down time.

After schooling Tommy once more, he entered the ring for his second round and unfortunately had a rail down leaving the ring with four faults.

There had been a clear ahead of him and another four-faulter so he was tying for second place with about eight horses to go. I threw a blanket over him and we watched the others go with four clear rounds in total to compete against the clock. One of them was Jean Goodwin on Nicki and it was going to be an exciting jump off. I remember Valma Craig was in the Jump Off as was a rider called Jane Poachin, also from Cheshire.

❃

It was so exciting to watch these riders and horses go against each other and Jean was last to go. Valma was leading with a clear in a good time and it was now all up to Jean as she came in and set off at an amazing pace. I could not believe how she cut the corners and before we knew it, was coming to the last fence. I remember as she drove Nicki on with her legs and he stood way off, however cleared the fence and raced through the finish, he knocked almost three seconds off Valma's time and won the class.

I remember the prize being thirty pounds, about fifty dollars, a lot of money in those days, though at that time these riders did not compete for the money. I remember they gave out eight rosettes and Tommy ended up with sixth. As far as I was concerned he won the class and I made sure that rosette was hanging in the window of the horsebox all the way home.

When we left the show ground that night, I knew I had entered another world and that day decided nothing would ever take me away from this dream which was becoming reality right in front of my eyes. I remember on the way home driving once again on the East Lancashire Road, we stopped for fish and chips. We walked in to the fish and chip shop and I was wearing my full riding outfit with Tommy's rosette pinned to my jacket. The people in the fish and chip shop were quite taken with us as they had never seen a horsebox outside before and thought we had famous racehorses in there.

❃

I could not contain myself as I told them much to Harry and Doreen's amusement that the horsebox contained a champion show jumper by the name of Caruso. As we drove home, I remember feeling tired, but the most contented I had ever felt and somehow knew that my life ahead was to become one of unbelievable adventure in the world of the horse, little did I know that day how much!

Chapter Five

It took a couple of days to come back down to earth, but it happened, although I knew I would never forget my first horse show as a groom. I did not get home that night until after eleven having bedded down the horses, fed them and saw that Tommy was comfortable after his day of competing in Cheshire.

I remember only so well jumping on my bicycle and riding home like the wind, I was in another world and nobody was going to bring me back to this one for quite a while. On arriving home, everyone was in bed; my family had no interest in horses whatsoever and thought I was an odd ball to be so involved. They really thought that this was going to be a passing phase and that pretty soon I would get on with my life without horses. Obviously they were wrong and eventually accepted that the horse had become a part of my life. At school, it was all I talked and wrote about in my essays, some were fascinated. Others quite bored and teased me. I didn't give a damn, I knew and nobody could phase my dreams of one day representing Great Britain on a British Show Jumping Team. I did not know at that time how fate would change my life and turn it completely around from the competing side to the commentary side, but it did.

❤

It was two weeks before Harry, Doreen and I set off for our next show and life at the stables continued as it had done, taking care of Tommy and Star. It was different now. I truly felt that I was totally involved in the Show Jumping World and that the world of riding schools was behind me, I was becoming a show jumper through and through. Our next show was to be also a one-day on the Saturday and from what I can remember, it was similar to the one at Cheadle Hulme with many of the same riders. I was so excited when it came around and had everything prepared just like I had done before. Doreen arrived with Harry and as she had the previous show, brought all kinds of wonderful goodies for us. I so enjoyed her sandwiches, cakes, different fruits and of course, her wonderful loving attitude to both Harry and I. She sort of mothered us and made sure we had everything to make our day such a special one.

I formed a special bond with Doreen and still today we are great friends and keep constantly in touch, hard to believe that was more than fifty years ago.

Harry brought the horsebox around and we loaded both horses this time, even though Star was not entered in the show. Harry wanted to introduce him to the excitement of the show ground with everything that was going on so that Star could settle and become familiar with everything before he was brought to compete.

CB

It took a little while to get him in the horsebox, even though we had loaded Tommy first. He eventually shot up the ramp and stood quietly next to his stable mate. They teased each other with little nips, head shaking and ears back and forth eventually settling down. There was a door from the living quarters of the horsebox into the horses' compartment so I could keep an eye on them. This calmed Star who was not used to traveling and once we started our journey, he neighed a little, until he finally settled.

I had given them both hay nets at either side of the compartment and this certainly helped. We drove for just over an hour and I remember Star being very excited on our arrival, he had never seen anything like it before. Being a Thoroughbred, he was a nervous type of animal to start with; he was just five and was trying to take it all in. I let Harry handle him totally at this show as he was quite a handful and was certainly too much for a twelve-year-old boy. Tommy could not care less and just stood outside the horsebox where we had tied him and continued to nibble on his hay net. Harry tacked up Star and I gave him a leg up, he'd just made it into the saddle before Star decided to leap in the air and have a very frisky buck. I was amazed at Harry staying on.

CB

I had never experienced a buck yet and hoped it would never happen to me. Little did I know that I would experience hundreds throughout my riding life, some depositing me on the ground with my pride totally ruined?

As Star and Harry left us, Doreen was a little nervous and told Harry to be careful. I remember him smiling and told her that she was only worried if something happened, as there would be nobody to drive the horsebox home. That was typical of Harry he had a cruel sense of humor with his sister and often teased her, as he did me. He played many tricks on me also and I will tell you about some of those, as we get deeper into the story. It took a while for him to settle Star down owing to the excitement and being a black horse, he lathered up quite quickly and became very sweaty. Fortunately, I had plenty of water and sponges in the horsebox including a sweat scraper, which I eventually had to use to wash him down and dry him off once Harry brought him back. It was starting to dawn on me now how hard it was to work shows, as I now had two horses in my care, which was quite a lot for a twelve-year-old with so little experience.

Of course, this taught me a tremendous amount at such an early age, something not many people had the fortune of having. I loved every minute of it and realized that these two horses were becoming my family, they definitely had become an extension of me and there was nothing I would not do for them.

೪

Today was not like the first show where I only had Tommy; this was a show that taught me what it meant to be a groom. I had the responsibility of two horses and I was going to make the most of it and be recognized for my hard work and dedication. I believe that Doreen and Harry realized that they had someone valuable on the team and I loved being with them. Having no fear of what I was doing became a tremendous help to me and gained me quite a bit of respect on the circuit very quickly. I did not realize it, but many of the other riders definitely noticed how hard I worked and some even had thoughts that one day when I grew up, I might even work for them, eventually, this did happen as you will see later.

Star eventually settled down and I cleaned the saddle and changed the girth for Tommy, though he did have his own bridle. Doreen had already been to the secretary and picked up Harry's number for the two classes that Tommy was in that day and I proceeded to get him ready for his first competition of the day. We put Star in the horsebox on the far side from the ramp, put it up and left it open a little so that the breeze would blow through and give Star some air. As Harry and I were leaving for the collecting ring with Tommy, Star decided to go crazy, he did not want Tommy to leave him so Doreen decided to stay with him until he settled, which he eventually did.

 og

On arrival at the collecting ring, there were many of the riders warming up for the class including some I had met in Cheadle Hulme. I felt on top of the world when they recognized me, and several of them, including Judy Ollerton, called me by name.

This was the ultimate to me and I totally felt that I had arrived in this tiny exclusive world of Show Jumping, I was so proud. The first competition for us that day was a speed class and really was not for Tommy, he was an Irish Hunter so a little heavier than a lot of the Thoroughbred's competing. Harry wanted him in there anyway as a warm up for the big class later that day and when it was his turn, he took Tommy around quite fast I thought, but he was not in the ribbons. It was a lot of fun though and I was quite amazed at how fast some of the riders rode the course, cutting corners like you would not believe and I heard several people saying about different horses, wow, that horse can turn on a sixpence. This was not said about Tommy of course but I knew of another Irish Hunter called Foxhunter ridden by Harry Llewelyn, together they had won an Olympic Gold Medal in Helsinki a few years before. Obviously this made me more proud for Tommy because I believed that one day he could do the same.

og

Of course, this was a dream and never happened, but in my mind, Tommy was definitely an Olympic horse and always would be to me. We took Tommy back to the horsebox and Doreen was still there with Star who was quite pleased to see Tommy coming back. Doreen made tea, brought out the sandwiches and cakes and we proceeded to have a little feast in the afternoon sun, it was heaven. We had tied Tommy to the outside of the horsebox and taken off his bridle, though we left his saddle on with a very loose girth and gave him a small amount of hay, he was very content. Star was much more settled now and we hoped he would remain that way later when we took Tommy to the arena for his main class of the day. A new experience for me was about to happen, as we came out of the horsebox, clouds had been forming to the west of us and it looked like rain. I said to Harry, will the jumping be cancelled, and he said, oh no, I have competed many times in the rain.

I hated rain, though as the years passed us by, I was to ride many times in all kinds of weather and learned to live with it, including competing. Each show was and always is, different, as was this. Doreen and I walked around while Harry took a nap and we saw many trade stands including one that sold crystal. I was fascinated by the colors and beauty in the glass and wished I could buy some.

ଔ

I was a twelve-year-old boy and did not have the money for crystal. Nevertheless, I swore that one day I would own some. Little did I know that I would become a collector and have some wonderful pieces?

Soon it was time to get back and get Tommy ready for the main competition of the day. We had to wake Harry, who was fast asleep on the sofa in the living area of the horsebox. While he got himself ready putting on his riding boots and tie, I prepared Tommy who was always the perfect gentleman with me, though he always laid his ears back and shook his head when I tightened up the girth.

This time, I rode him down to the collecting ring and Harry said he would join me down there. I felt so proud riding him and this was the first time all the other riders had seen me on a horse. I was starting to pay attention to how they sat, walked, trotted and cantered and this was to be a great learning arena for me. I wanted to be like them all, however, I also wanted to be unique in my riding becoming the best in the country, maybe the world, this was my dream. I dismounted when Harry arrived and gave him a leg up and off he rode on Tommy, how I wished it was me but I had not yet had any real jumping experience by then and was certainly not ready for competition.

ଔ

I was also not old enough to ride in adult competitions and in those days, if you were tall, you had to receive special permission from the British Show Jumping Association to compete with the adults and in most cases one had to wear a weighted saddle pad. The minimum weight for men was eleven stone eleven pounds and I believe eleven stone for the women. It was time to school Tommy over the practice jumps and there were always at least two, sometimes three in the collecting ring. Everyone of course was using them and we always had to be patient for our turn in altering the heights and spreads, or widths, as they are known now. Quite often though, many of the riders jumped the same fences that had been set by another rider so it all balanced out in the end. That day was not that great for us as Tommy had two fences down in the first round so we did not make the jump off. This meant that we wouldn't be staying around so we packed everything up and headed home. I felt quite disappointed having desperately wanting to see the main class of the day and all the other riders, however, I dare not show my disappointment and smiled thanking Harry and Doreen again as we left the show ground for a wonderful day. By the time we arrived home, fed and bedded the horses down for the night and I set off home it was still daylight.

I still rode home on my bicycle feeling like a million dollars.

ভ

Always riding home on my bicycle from a show in my full riding outfit, I often wondered how many drivers in cars and people I passed thought that I was somebody famous from the Show Jumping world. Looking back, I doubt anybody even gave me a second look or noticed, though I will never know.

Chapter Six

As the show season continued, we had been to several one-day events and the excitement was building now as the first three-day show was looming up for us in a week. It was to be in Manchester and I had never been to a three day show before, I could not believe my excitement after Doreen telling me that quite a few of the top International Riders would be there. My heart and mind raced wondering if I would get to meet any of them or if they would actually speak to me!

The show was to be held on a Thursday, Friday and Saturday, very few, if any, shows in those days were held on a Sunday. I was already on holiday for the summer from school so that was not a problem and we would be driving there and home each of the three days so I had a lot to prepare. It was just over an hour's drive each way and on the first day it felt like we were driving forever, I so wanted to be there. As we approached the show ground, I could not believe its enormity and I was even more amazed that there was more than one arena. I had not seen this before including the number of marquees; they seemed to go on forever.

↊

Then I saw it and got the chills as we pulled into the show ground, the rows of temporary stables that had been put up for the horses, wow. I could not believe it and noticed so many riders schooling, grooms rushing back and forth doing their chores for magnificent horses like I had never seen before.

Then I spotted some beautiful custom horseboxes that people were living in, dogs running around. There were some beautiful cars and rows of caravans that had been brought in by many of the riders. Now this was another world and I started to find out what the true show jumping world was all about, a family of people who travelled all over the country together at these enormous shows. Some of these people were on the road for weeks at a time and I wanted this now, here were some of the cream of our sport, I was about to be introduced to something beyond belief. Of course, it was not possible to join this elite group yet, I was still at school but I ached to be a part of this amazing set of celebrity riders, horses and total talent filled with the excitement of fame and competition. Now the true meaning of International Show Jumping was right in front of me and I was in awe!

As we parked our horsebox in the daily parking area, I did not know what to do first. I felt like a person possessed and just wanted to explore every inch of this amazing new world.

⟡

I wanted to be engulfed by it all and never to leave it again. My heart was racing and Doreen sensed this, she wanted me to enjoy it also and offered to take me on a tour of the stables. Off we set and suddenly this gorgeous Thoroughbred horse's head popped out over a stable door and I heard a man's voice from the other side. Doreen immediately shouted, as she often did to me; "Ello Darlin" as this man's head appeared. I was introduced to him, his name was Sammy Morphet from Woolton near Liverpool and his beautiful horse was called Derek. Sammy was a character and I was to learn that he was one of Harvey Smiths' best friends. I could hardly contain myself knowing that Harvey was one of the most famous riders in the world and would be arriving any minute with his team of top international horses.

Could this be real and happening to me, was I dreaming or was I about to be in the presence of Harvey Smith? All sorts of things were going through my head such as, will Harvey even notice me, will he speak to me and will I get close enough to be even in the same space as him? I was soon to find out and somehow knew that Sammy would make it alright. I never even imagined at that time that Harvey and his wife Irene would become good friends with me, one day being their guest to dinner. Sammy gave Doreen a kiss and we continued our tour around the stables and Doreen seemed to know almost everybody we came into contact with.

⟡

Little did I know that she, Harry and their sister Joan had competed against most of these riders growing up and they had all been friends for years.

37

Jean Goodwin was there with Nicki and Hobo, Judy Ollerton with her horses, Valma Craig, Carol Beard, David Boston Barker and his brother William who would soon be representing Great Britain on an Olympic Team. Then this magnificent horse looked out at us and Doreen said, do you know who that is? I did not until she told me it was the great Pegasus, owned by Mrs. Chambers and ridden by the great British rider, Ted Williams. I had seen the two on television several times and everything was starting to become too much. From my humble background, was this really happening to me, would my friends at school ever believe me? I wanted everyone I knew to see me so that they, like me would realize that all of this was real. Now I truly believed that there was nothing in this world could ever take me away from this dream that was quickly becoming reality.

I did not realize at the time I was entering the history of our wonderful sport and one day would be able to tell the world an incredible story that only dreams to most young people would become a reality. The visions of my dreams were unfolding before my eyes. The riders and horses that would make show jumping what it is today were starting to come into my life right there, and this was just the beginning.

CB

The Manchester show in the early sixties was one of the biggest three-day shows in the country attracting many of Britain's top riders. As the three days progressed, I was to see quite a few more and just casually say hello to some. The Lanni brothers came from Doncaster in Yorkshire, John and Carmen, they were related to the Masserellas who owned Mister Softee. Jane Poachin was there, she was from Cheshire. She owned and rode Tamarisk Cottage and would eventually marry Carmen Lanni.

John Bailey who would win the junior European Championship with Dominick came from Scotland, Andrew Fielder came with Vibart and Rocket from Pool in Wharfedale, Yorkshire. Andrew; eventually becoming one of our top International riders was the winner of the Leading Show Jumper of the Year at the Horse of the Year Show. He was the youngest ever to achieve this, beating all of the top riders in Europe. How could I know that he would eventually become my best friend? Malcolm Pyrah was also there riding then for Trevor Banks, Trevor was the guy who sold Goodwill to H.R.H. Princess Anne, the horse she rode on the Olympic team in Montreal. Malcolm would go on to win the Rome Grand Prix on April Love and one day become the chairman of the British Show Jumping Association, the governing body of our sport in Great Britain.

CR

Jean Goodwin was at that time crazy about Malcolm though he would marry Judy Boulter while Jean married the steeplechase jockey, Stephen Davenport.

Judy Boulter was one of our most successful riders and won many of the big classes throughout Great Britain. Lionel Dunning was at Manchester that week with his top horses and he would eventually become one of our most famous International riders, his most successful horse being Jungle Bunny. He married Pam Couldron, another great rider and they had a son who also became a show jumper now breeding horses in Lincolnshire. Ted Edgar was there with his international horse called Jane Summers; this was before he married Liz Broome, the sister of David. David Broom was already an Olympian and would also go on to become the men's European and World Show Jumping Champion, not to mention one of the most successful riders of all time in the world. Ken and Stephen Pritchard from Staffordshire became very good friends of mine some years later. Shirley Edwards with Laramie, one of our leading lady riders who rode for Britain on several teams, and the list goes on.

This was the most memorable day and most exciting of my life being an exceptional experience to a twelve-year-old boy. This was even more amazing as a lot of these riders had already been on television and some were household names already.

CR

Even my parents knew some of those names and I wondered if they would believe that I had just spent the day with them. Many more of those days were to come and as time went by, I was to get to know these celebrities and the thrill was almost indescribable when they started to address me by my name, wow, these people new me, Frank Waters, they actually knew me.

It was not long before Doreen brought me back to earth and informed me that it was time to get Tommy ready for his class. We headed back to the horsebox and as often happened; there was Harry fast asleep on the sofa snoring his head off. He was a very laid back kind of guy and very little daunted Harry, though he was amused at my enthusiasm to all of this.

He was getting to know me well enough now that he constantly teased me and often played some pretty mean tricks including sending me to a hardware store to buy a can of striped paint to paint the show jumps. I of course fell for it and tried my hardest to inform the salesperson that it did exist and that he must have been stupid as I was involved with show jumping and this was the only way to paint the jumps. What a laugh they must have had on me and Harry cried with laughter when he found out that I actually tried to buy this. Another time, he sent me to the store for a can of elbow grease, this was to put an incredible shine on Tommy's coat, of course, I go back to the same store and ask for Blackman's Elbow Grease.

ഗ

Once again, everyone in the store had a great laugh on me, I think Harry was a bit of a sadist, maybe he was just a large child at heart full of mischief, but we will never know.

Doreen still laughs like crazy when I remind her of the striped paint and elbow grease; those were the days!

At this particular Manchester show, we had several of the regional championships, hence the tremendous turnout of top riders and it was exciting for me as Tommy was to be competing in a couple of these events. We had also brought Star to ride in one of the novice events so a busy day lay ahead for me having to prepare two show jumpers for competition. Quite a task for a twelve-year-old boy but I was more than ready and wanted to go home with all the trophies I could. The novice class was first of the day and was a Foxhunter competition for Star with fences at no more than 3' 6". We warmed up Star and he seemed to be settling quite well, however, was a little distracted in the arena and had two fences down accumulating eight faults. Harry was pleased, as he knew that Star would only get better with time.

Now it was time to warm up Tommy and get him ready for one of the big events of the day. This was my time as my heart was definitely with Tommy and I wanted him to win it all and beat everyone. I tacked him up and rode him down to the collecting ring and who should be riding around on Warpaint, Harvey Smith?

ഗ

I could not take my eyes off him and kept looking for Sammy hoping he would introduce me, sadly, he was not to be seen and I had to snap out of it as my stare was becoming rude, though I am sure Harvey was used to this from so many people around the country. Harry appeared and after giving him a leg up, he trotted off on Tommy and as he rode past Harvey, I heard him say, "afternoon Harvey" and Harvey acknowledged him. I was shocked as Harry never let on who he knew. It turned out that they were just acquaintances, however, Harvey knew who Harry was and that was good enough for me.

I walked into the middle of the collecting ring ready to build the practice jumps for Harry and could not believe that I was actually feet away from the great Harvey Smith. I guess looking back, it was all a little silly, in those days these top show jumping riders were almost as famous as the sixties pop stars. 'If a person knew the Beatles, then they also knew Harvey Smith, he was literally a household name'. I didn't get to formally meet him at that show nevertheless, it did happen soon enough. After several practice jumps it was time to take Tommy to the entrance of the arena and there was Curly Beard acting as collecting ring steward once again, cracking jokes and making everyone laugh.

 (3

Curly knew everyone and all of the riders had a lot of respect for him. I heard him telling Harry that he was next to go and Doreen took her place beside me as Harry and Tommy entered the arena.

I remember it was a lovely day and at all of the shows in England in those days, the horses jumped on grass. The judges rang the bell and Tommy set off with Harry through the start with Doreen and me nervous as ever. I truly believe that Tommy always wanted to do well for me and to our delight, jumped a superb first clear round which put him into the jump off. There were about forty horses in the class and there had already been three clears with more than twenty to go. The next round was timed, however, not against the clock, that would be for the second round of clears. I do not remember how many rosettes the show was giving out but I do know that the first round finished with about twelve clear rounds of which I remember Harvey was one on Warpaint, Jean Goodwin on Nicki and Malcolm Pyrah on Mr. Whippy, three of the top horses in the class. I don't remember the others but I knew we had some very tough competition in the next round.

It was a drawn first round jump off and Tommy was second to go, we could not believe it. He jumped another clear which put him into the final round against the clock. Warpaint and Nicki also jumped clear but Mr. Whippy had a fence down with four faults.

ഗ

I believe seven horses jumped clear and headed into the final round against the clock, my Tommy was one of them. The tension was unbelievable as Tommy was not really in the league of Warpaint and Nicki and he really tried his heart out but had two fences down with eight faults. Both Harvey on Warpaint and Jean on Nicki jumped clear with Harvey having the fastest time and he won the class with Jean second on Nicki. I believe Tommy was fifth, which was an amazing day for him, and I remember Harry could not have been more pleased. That was the only class they had entered that day but Harry decided we would stay to watch the big Grand Prix and for the first time in my life I watched in awe as Harvey came out on the great O'Malley.

Now this combination of horse and rider were one of the best in the world and to watch them live for the first time was unbelievable, needless to say, they won the class with amazing riding skills cutting corners like you would not believe and received a large trophy presented by the Mayor of Manchester with a check for two hundred and fifty pounds, a fortune in those days. We left the show ground about six and headed home, I did not want to go and could have stayed there forever. My only consolation was that I would be back the following day and sat quietly all the way home dreaming of never going back to school and becoming a full time member of this never to be forgotten crowd of amazing celebrity riders and horses.

ഗ

I actually slept in the horsebox that night wishing it was on the show ground in Manchester with all the riders and grooms, I wanted it so badly to be a part of that world and to enjoy it to the fullest.

I dreamt of what the following day would bring and wondered if this time Tommy would be the big winner beating them all to become the champion, we shall see!

Chapter Seven

Having slept in the horsebox, I didn't get a lot of sleep and was up with the horses at around five the next morning. It was starting to get light so I fed them, mucked out the stalls and then started to clean the tack and get everything ready for our departure that morning to the Manchester Show. I wondered whom I would see today and that I would leave the ordinary world behind once again as we drove through the show ground gate into my world of top class show jumping.

It was getting toward 7 a.m. and Doreen had left some cereal, milk and drinks in the horsebox for me and I proceeded to have breakfast.

I could hardly eat with excitement and knew that we still had two hours to go before we left for Manchester. At eight o'clock I started to get the horses ready for their journey, Star was also coming with us today and he was getting a little better travelling and seemed to take his cue from Tommy. I wrapped both horses' legs and put on their tail bandages followed by their sweat blankets, which they travelled in. I then fastened a head collar (halter) on to both the horses and then let the ramp down from the horsebox. It was just a few minutes later that Harry drove into the stable yard with Doreen, I was surprised to see Mrs. Priestley, their mother who was coming with us today.

ᘓ

She was a wonderful lady and always had a smile on her face, laughed a lot and had a wonderful sense of humor. Now I know where Harry got his from, he teased her a lot and it was obvious that they had a very special bond.

As always, Doreen had plenty of bags with her full of goodies that we would consume throughout the day, I always looked forward to her special treats and wondered what they would be today!

I brought Tommy out of his stall, he was never a problem loading into the horsebox and once he was in Harry brought out Star who by now seeing Tommy, rushed up the wooden ramp, neighed and started to settle down. We always made sure they had hay nets each as this occupied them on their journey. Harry and I pushed up and locked the ramp in place and we then helped Mrs. Priestley up into the front cab giving her the prime seat. Doreen and I travelled in the back, which pleased me as when we did this, she would bring out her gourmet sandwiches and we would have our own little feast back there. At that time, Doreen had a Boxer dog called Peggy and she was with us today, she proceeded to stare us down while drooling wanting pieces of our sandwiches.

We had a couple of big sliding windows in the living quarters that opened both slightly, which gave us a cool fresh breeze through the living quarters.

ଔ

Peggy settled down and fell asleep on her big pillow on the floor and Doreen proceeded to give Harry and her mum some hot tea and a sandwich through the door to the cab. It still was a pure novelty to me watching all of this unfold right before me, as it was still fairly new. They, of course had done this for many years and it was second nature to them. I think they all got a kick out of watching me taking it all in. Mrs. Priestley and I enjoyed our time together with lots of laughter. I think she liked having a younger boy around again to look after and she certainly did that, I really grew to love her.

Pretty soon I started to recognize the neighborhood of the Manchester show and we were soon on the show ground.

It seemed busier today and it was, especially as we were now going into the weekend with lots more of the public coming out to see the wonderful tents full of everything from massive flower displays to the tent full of home baked goods from ladies far and wide. Most had come to see the stars of our sport, the show jumpers, the horses and riders. Many of the kids and some adults had autograph books and would be going home with treasured signatures from our many riders including some of our most famous.

ଔ

On entering the show ground, there was a uniformed man today directing the horseboxes to their designated parking area and I could see all of the temporary stables not so far away. I so wanted our horses to be stabled there but this never happened with the Priestley's, I had to wait a few years before I would experience this with "my" horses being stabled on a show ground with me taking care of them.

Once Harry parked we let the ramp down slightly to give the horses some air and I asked Doreen if we could walk out to the stables. She smiled and said of course we could, however, this time Mrs. Priestley would come with us, and boy was she respected by the show jumping crowd. Harry of course would curl up and take his usual nap; we always said that he could sleep on a washing line. Mrs. Priestley slid her arm through Doreen's and off we walked toward paradise, the walkway of the stars as I called it. On the way I realized just how many people knew and came to say hello to Mrs. Priestley, and Doreen of course. She had travelled the circuit with the kids when they were growing up and many of the riders had grown up knowing her as one of the great mothers of our sport. Her first name was Miriam and quite a few people addressed her as that, until she died many years later, I always called her Mrs. Priestley.

ᘓ

Who did we bump into down at the stables? Sammy Morphet with Deric, my heart almost stopped, he was sitting on a bale of straw talking to his best friend, Harvey Smith. Harvey had his horses right next to Deric and his groom also called Doreen but known to the show jumping world as Blossom was busy taking care of them and getting them ready for competition. I could not believe how thorough she was and her many years of experience showed. It was all second nature to her and everything she did seemed effortless. Sammy got up and gave both Doreen and Mrs. Priestley a hug and Harvey said hello to them and asked, 'so who is this young whipper snapper then?' I looked around not believing he was referring to me and I felt my face burning. Doreen smiled and introduced me; I didn't know what to say as Harvey tussled his hand through my hair and asked me how old I was. I answered him and he then introduced me to Blossom. Blossom and I actually became good friends as the season drew on.

Blossom had four horses with her: O'Malley, Harvester, Warpaint and The Sea Hawk, who was probably the best speed horse that ever lived. Sea Hawk also had a mean streak and very few could get close to him, except Blossom of course, he would not think twice about giving you a nasty bite and he seemed a little more 'testy' with younger people.

ᘓ

Of course, I could not believe that I had just met Harvey Smith, the greatest and most famous rider in England, and certainly known then throughout the world. I wanted to be sixteen right there and then and to work for him with Blossom, perhaps even be taught by him to be one of Britain's top show jumping riders, boy, did I have it bad. I knew that at least four more years of school were ahead of me, but I wanted to leave right there and then running away to the world that I wanted to be a part of so bad full time. I did not care if I never had another day off in my life as long as I was at horse shows with my horses.

Many more of the riders came up and spoke with Mrs. Priestley seeing her for the first time this year. Curly Beard, the collecting ring steward seemed delighted to see her and she him, they ended up laughing like crazy after big hugs and it was obvious they had known each other for a very long time with great mutual respect. Soon it was time to head back to the horsebox and get Star ready for the Foxhunter competition, this was a qualifier for the Regionals and those placed in the top three at Regionals would go on to the finals at the Horse of the Year Show. It was a big class today with more than fifty horses competing, Star was still not all that experienced and he really did not have the scope to go on and become a top show jumper.

છ

Show jumping was really just a hobby for Harry and he really didn't have the inspiration to go on to become a top rider; he did this purely for fun and enjoyment.

I look back now and realize that it was the perfect arena for me to gain experience and learn the ropes at an un-pressured level gaining more knowledge, as the season got deeper.

After tacking up Star, giving Harry a leg up we headed for the collecting ring, which was much bigger than the shows we had already attended. After schooling Star for about twenty minutes, Harry let Curly know that he was ready to enter the arena for his first round. Curly wrote Harry's back number on the board telling him that he was about five out. By then, Doreen and Mrs. Priestley had arrived ready to support him in competition and see just how he would do with Star. Some of the top riders had young horses in the Foxhunter competition and this in those days was where most novice horses started their future career. Curly called Harry and he cantered into the arena and we could not believe it, with all of the hustle and bustle of a big show, Star stopped at the first fence.

CB

Back in those days, it was three faults for a refusal and there had already been about six clears with a lot of horses to go. We knew that Star would not be in the jump off that day but he did complete the course with a rail down and sometime faults as well. We took him back to the horsebox and it was still a couple of hours before Tommy's class so Doreen decided to get lunch ready and the kettle was put on. The living quarters of the horsebox was in the middle and we had another single horse stall at the back. Doreen had put a picnic table and chairs in there which we set up outside on the grass, she set it up and today was going to be a picnic lunch. I was surprised that a couple of the riders stopped by for a cup of tea and a biscuit, which is a cookie as they say in the U.S. This is a common thing in England; people are always stopping by for a cuppa.

Apart from the wonderful sandwiches, Doreen had baked this amazing sponge cake from scratch with Jam and fresh cream filling, I wanted to eat the whole thing it looked so good. The table now fully set, a pot of tea made we sat down to a wonderful picnic lunch and life could not be better. When we had finished, I helped Doreen take everything into the horsebox and helped her wash up before we had a walk to the flower tent, Doreen's favorite.

CB

I couldn't believe how big the marquee was and the flower arrangements were magnificent with every type of bloom imaginable. The arrangements were from about ten flowers to more than fifty in some of the displays, they were absolutely magnificent and it was hard to believe people could actually make a display of flowers look so beautiful. Doreen had brought her camera and photographed quite a few of the arrangements and I knew she would want to try and copy some of them at home.

They had a beautiful large English garden in the back and grew some of the most spectacular blooms which she would often cut and arrange magnificently in the house. We eventually walked back to the horsebox and were very surprised to see Doreen and Harry's father Mr. Priestley had arrived in his beautiful big Rover. He had decided to join us watch Harry compete on Tommy that afternoon. Doreen made him a cup of tea and a couple of sandwiches followed by a delicious piece of that sponge cake. I was desperate for another piece but dare not ask, Doreen sensed this, there really was not that much left, however, gave me the last piece, I was in heaven and could not thank her enough. Mr. Priestley was a very nice man, although I never quite felt as comfortable with him as I did with Mrs. Priestley, she was just like a mother to me and made me feel totally at ease.

ੴ

Obviously, Mr. & Mrs. Priestley spent the rest of the afternoon together and it turned out he had a members pass to the pavilion. That is where they headed, he liked to have a Scotch and a cigarette so off they went and found perfect seats to watch the rest of the day's show jumping. We did not see Mrs. Priestley again that day as she drove home in the Rover with her husband, which put Doreen and me in the cab with Harry on the way home. Pretty soon, it was time to get Tommy ready for the Grand Prix and we felt excited for him, as he had already jumped the day before so was pretty used to the atmosphere on the show ground.

Chapter Eight

At this particular Manchester show as mentioned earlier, quite a few of the Regional championships had been scheduled over these three days and this particular Grand Prix was to incorporate the Northern Championship. Because of this we had more than fifty in the class and many or our best horses and riders had come to compete including the great Harvey Smith. There was a tremendous amount of excitement owing to the fact that one of these super horses and riders would be crowned the North of England Champion today, we all wondered who that would be and if Harvey would take the trophy. Tommy was his usual self and just seemed to take it all in stride and just stood for me while I got him ready for the competition.

With the help of Doreen, I learned a little about braiding today and she showed me how to do this, as we call it in England, plait his mane, boy, did he look special.

I gave him an extra grooming and his tack was shining, this was to be as far as I was concerned, his introduction to the large crowd that had come out today to watch the competition. Harry allowed me to ride him down to the collecting ring and I was proud as punch considering that a twelve-year-old was taking this amazing, great looking horse down to competition, how I wished it was me riding him in that championship!

CB

Harry with all the other riders in the competition had already walked the course and it looked enormous to me, most of the jumps being bigger than I was. I had walked the course with Harry and was amazed at how big it was. It was built today by one of our leading course designers at the time, Alan Ball. Alan was known for his courses all over Europe and was the official course designer for the Royal International Horse Show and the Horse of the Year Show.

As we rode through the many people lining the pathway to the collecting ring, I felt so proud of Tommy being watched by the show jumping fans including several asking me who he was. Many wanted to touch him and gave him a little stroke or pat as we continued toward the collecting ring. Harry was closely behind us with Doreen and several people in the crowd, not knowing who Harry was stopped him and asked for his autograph, he loved it, as did I. I saw some rather puzzled faces as they looked at the signature probably asking themselves, "who is this guy", they were soon to find out when he would enter this big arena as a competitor in the North of England Grand Prix Championship. The support that the general public gives to equestrian events in Britain is amazing, I only wish that it were the same here in the United States, what a thrill it would be for our riders to have an enormous fan base and a loyal following week after week.

❦

As I reached the collecting ring, I could see several of the top riders warming up their horses, Harvey Smith, Jean Goodwin, John Bailey, Johnny Greenwood, Jane Poachin, John Lanni, Carol Beard and others all on top horses, some that had represented Great Britain in Nations Cups around the world. I reluctantly got off Tommy giving Harry a leg up and proudly proceeded over to the practice jumps with Doreen. We had to take our turn as so many were using the three jumps that had been allocated to the collecting ring. In the meantime, Harry slowly trotted and cantered Tommy around to loosen him up and to make sure that he was supple enough before he started to jump. Pretty soon it was our turn to take over a couple of the jumps, a vertical and a decent spread which we proceed to lower a little after one of the riders had finished their schooling.

Harry always started Tommy off slowly before we increased the heights; it helped him get used to the particular fences and also to limber up as we raised them to competition height. Tommy was about six or seven out and Curly had him on the board and as always was running the competition like clockwork. We never had down time in England; the competitions always ran beautifully so that the viewing public would not be sitting around looking at an empty arena.

❦

If it ever happened that we had no horses at the gate, the announcer would always let the riders know that they had 30 seconds to have a horse in the arena or else the class would be closed. I never saw this

50

happen, all of our competitors knew that this was the silent rule and showed up pronto! The announcer in those days was a man from Chester called Jim Milton. He had a mobile unit with several speakers on the roof and always showed up at the big events in the north of England.

I was often envious of him as many of the top riders would go and sit with him and chat for what seemed hours during competitions.

So far there had been around five or six clear rounds and we were about a third way through the competition and Tommy was two out. Doreen and I left Harry to ponder with Tommy and we wished them every bit of luck in the world and took our spot at the side of the arena. In a class of this size we had no idea what to expect though I believe Harry was far more nervous today than Tommy. Like all professionals, he knew how to focus on the job at hand the minute he entered the arena and suddenly, there he was coming through the gate on my beloved Tommy. Mr. Milton announced him, "Next to go is Harry Priestley riding Caruso from Southport here in Lancashire." The judges rang the bell and off they rode through the start with both Doreen's and my tummy in knots.

CR

Half way around the course he was still clear and then he came to the big combination, it seemed enormous and I remember Doreen grabbing my arm. He jumped the first part beautifully, then the big spread in the middle then what seemed like the biggest jump I had ever seen, the large spread, he took off and gave the rail a hard knock but it stayed to our relief. He was now about six jumps from home and still clear, our hearts were in our mouths as he was still clear with just two to go. I could see he was pulling a little and Harry was checking his strides as he came in to the last fence which was a large upright, he seemed to get a little close, twisted a little and sailed over for a clear round. Doreen and I could hardly contain ourselves. I actually thought she was going to be sick. She had tears in her eyes and told me that this was the biggest course Tommy had every jumped and certainly the biggest competition he had every competed in.

Harry came out of the ring with an enormous smile and all of the riders around the gate were congratulating him. I had an enormous handful of fresh grass for Tommy and he eagerly snatched it from me. He was sweating but I did not care and gave him the biggest hug imaginable and as Harry dismounted he actually showed Tommy some wonderful affection, which was nice to see. From what I remember, this was about the eighth clear round in the class and still a lot to go.

છ

I threw on Tommy's sweat rug and walked him around until he cooled off while Harry and Doreen watched some riders go; then I walked Tommy back to the horsebox.

With all the excitement we had almost forgotten about Star who was due to compete in the Foxhunter class in the smaller ring, Harry decided to withdraw him today and just concentrate on the big class with Tommy.

He did ride Star up to the collecting ring though and gave him a little schooling, which was part of his education as a young horse and gained him a little more experience on the show ground. This was a wonderful test for him as the show was so big with two huge rings, we had horses all over the place and with the public showing up, this was another piece of the pie for Star to get used to.

Of course, I constantly made an enormous fuss of Tommy and made sure that he had everything he needed which included sponging him down with some cold water after taking his tack off. It would be at least another hour before he had to go back for his first jump off so I gave him some water and a little hay. He just took it all in stride and I was never more proud of him than at that moment, I prayed that this would be his day and he would win the class. Suddenly Mr. & Mrs. Priestley pulled up in the Rover having been stuck in traffic and could not believe they had missed Tommy's first round.

છ

Of course, they were thrilled to discover that he had made the jump off, Mr. Priestley gave Tommy a cigarette to chew on, he often did this; then Mr. and Mrs. Priestley headed for the members pavilion for lunch and to watch the rest of the class and the all-important jump off. Just as they were leaving Mrs. Priestley gave me a hug and told me how beautiful Tommy looked, this made me feel wonderful as I thought so too, it was nice to hear it from somebody else.

Pretty soon, Harry asked me if I would go down to the collecting ring and ask Curly how many more there were to go in the first round so off I set and at quite a pace. Curly was his usual funny self and when I approached him he asked me, "what do you need scowser?" I smiled and politely told him that Harry wanted to know how many were left in the first round. He sent me over to the board and said, "if you can count, see for yourself." He was always teasing but I counted how many were left and headed back to tell Harry, it was about eight.

Harry knew that they would need some time to set for the jump off course and I proceeded to tack up Tommy once again having already cleaned his saddle and bridle and groomed him ready for this important part of the competition. This time Harry rode him down to the collecting ring and I was following behind carrying the grooming kit, Doreen was at my side.

೮೮

She was an absolute trooper and always had an armful of stuff, the sweat rug, the grooming attire and anything else that Harry may need including most of the time, his riding hat. I tried to wear it once and they laughed as it fell down over my face, it was far too big for me. Now remember, in those days most of the riders warmed up without wearing their hat, it was only mandatory in the arena and they all jumped outside without a safety helmet.

On arrival at the collecting ring, we discovered that there would be about eleven in the first jump off so I knew we had a fighting chance.

In this class, they had twelve rosettes so I knew Tommy would get at least one of those. We were also surprised to discover that Harvey had only one of his three horses through, Harvester, the other two had both knocked a rail down so were out of the competition. Jean Goodwin was in there with Nicki as was John Bailey with Dominick, the junior European Champions, and Ted Edgar with Jane Summers, a horse he had won the King George V Gold cup on. This was amazing, Tommy was up against these amazing horses and riders and I knew he had as good a chance as any of them. In show jumping, anything can happen on a given day and this one was going to be no exception. I guess looking back, Tommy was probably one of the oldest horses in the competition as he was fourteen then, nevertheless; he still had a few good years left in him for a show jumper.

೮೮

Harry was working Tommy quietly in the corner of the collecting ring and seemed to be talking to him. I knew Tommy was listening, he was one of the most intelligent horses I knew and I always thought he understood everything we said to him. In those days, the riders got to walk the first jump off course so off they went into the arena and I walked Tommy around whispering in his ear that he was going to win this for me. As the riders came out, I gave Harry a leg up and we headed over to the jumps, he was eighth to go so we had a little time for practice jumps before we had to head over to the ring. Curly was getting everybody together and was joking around with them all as usual, it was his way of making the riders feel relaxed, he was an expert at that and was very much respected by everyone. I could not believe the size of the crowd that had gathered around the arena to watch this class and even more came to see the jump off.

Apart from the people leaning up against the arena fence, the stands were also full as was the member's enclosure, hardly any elbow room at all. This of course added tremendous atmosphere to the event and it was the first time I had experienced anything like it. I can remember feeling nervous, excited and very important that my horse, Tommy was in this jump off with all of these people going to see him try his best for Harry, Doreen and myself.

 og

Not to forget also Harry's parents who happened to be watching from the member's enclosure.

I remember the first to go was Curly's daughter Carol on Mayfly; she had won 'Leading Show Jumper of the Year' at the Horse of the Year Show. Carol entered the arena and much to the shock of everyone, Mayfly fell at one of the fences and I remember Carol hurting her arm and had to leave the arena.

She also had mud on her face, I remember Curly saying to her "Didn't I tell you to wash your face and hands before you left the house" everyone including Carol laughed as Curly always meant well. In those days you did not get eliminated for a fall, it was eight faults if a horse or rider fell and you could continue if you wished. Carol was checked out and a part from a strain was fine, these show jumpers are tough and it takes a lot to put them completely out of competition. I have known them ride with broken collarbones, shoulders, arms strapped up and all sorts of injuries. It is a tough sport and the only one where men and women compete on an equal level. In fact, a British rider, Pat Smythe was the first lady ever to compete in an Olympic Games and she won a bronze medal in Stockholm, 1956.

Next go was John Bailie on Dominic and he jumped a super clear round to give us our first clear in the jump off, then came Jean with Nicki and had a fence down, so John was the only clear so far.

ဆ

I remember Harvey being third or fourth on Harvester and he jumped as expected a beautiful clear so we knew there was going to be an exciting jump off. A couple more jumped off with no clears then Ted Edgar came in with Jane Summers and proceeded to give us our third clear. Now it was Tommy's turn, Doreen and I were so nervous neither of us could stand still and Curly let me stand in his booth which gave me a little more height to watch. Doreen was at the arena entrance and suddenly the judges rang the bell and Tommy set off. As he jumped the first fence, he actually gave a little bit of a buck, which I had not seen him do before. Doreen was to tell me later that when he felt good, he often did this and was his way of saying, I am ready for this. He continued to jump magnificently around the course and was approaching the last two fences and was clear so far.

As he approached the last but one fence from home I remember Curly saying to Doreen, I have never seen Tommy jump this well before and I hoped he had not jinxed him. He had not as Tommy sailed over the last two jumps with convincing style and flew through the finish with a clear round. I think from what I can remember, I almost fell head over heels out of Curly's booth and Doreen and I both could not stop jumping up and down, the cheers from the crowd was amazing.

ဆ

Harry came out of the arena smiling like a Cheshire cat with a grin from eye to eye, he could not be happier and kidded with me that he would not take Tommy to the knacker's yard, he was always teasing me about that one, never meant it of course. We now had four clear rounds with three to go and I prayed that none of them would go clear which was pretty mean, this was an important event and everybody wanted to win it. One of the three was William Barker riding North Flight and he jumped a clear also giving us the fifth clear round.

Suddenly, that first jump off was over, the judges drew who would go in what order and Tommy was drawn fourth in the final jump off.

A couple of jumps were removed from the first jump off and this left us with the final jump off course against the clock, I don't think I have ever been more excited in my life. Here was my horse, my beloved Tommy in a jump off with some of the greatest horses and riders in England, I was not riding him, yet felt like a star. Ted Edgar was the first to go on Jane Summers and he raced around the course in a very fast time, he was trying to set the standard, however, had two rails down for eight faults. Then came John Bailey on Dominic who was not quite as fast as Ted, but he had a rail for four faults and took the lead. Two away from Tommy as Harvey came in on Harvester, everyone knew how skillful he was against the clock and could turn a horse on a dime.

CR

He flew around that course almost turning in the air at every jump but turned too sharply into one of the spread fences and Harvester just clipped it in front for a rail down. He did however, by far knock seconds off the other two times and with his very fast time took the lead. As Harry came in with Tommy, everyone knew he was the underdog and Curly spoke quietly telling Harry to take it easy and go for a clear. As I have mentioned, Tommy was not the fastest horse against the clock and had nothing to lose. Harry seemed to have an air of equanimity about him today as he set off around the course at a faster pace than normal, however did not race as the other riders had done. He jumped a magnificent round and as he came to the last two fences you could hear a slight murmur coming from the crowd, Tommy sailed over the last but one and was about five strides from the last and as he approached it, people were starting to stand and both Doreen and I had our hearts in our mouths.

As Tommy approached the last fence his ears were so pricked, I could see Harry holding him to get his stride right and they met it perfectly sailing over for the first clear round with just one to go. The crowd erupted with applause and cheered like you could not believe and Doreen burst into tears. She hugged me so hard I remember Harry throwing his hat in the air as all of the other riders already started congratulating us.

CR

Now there was still one to go so you can imagine the tension as William Barker came into the arena on North Flight and often the last rider on course in show jumping has the advantage knowing that nobody will follow. It gives them the opportunity to take risks and they have learned from what the other riders before them have done over this jump off course. Doreen and I could not watch as we heard the bell for William to start his course, this was it and we knew that he could beat Tommy's time though North Flight was also a fairly big horse like Tommy and not the greatest speed horse in the class.

We heard a few oohs and aahs as he rode the course and suddenly we heard a large sigh of disappointment as a rail came down. I could not believe it, he was at least six seconds faster than Tommy and we were amazed that North Flight clipped the rail on the very last fence and had it down for four faults. Doreen looked at me and screamed, I don't believe it, I don't believe it, Harry and Tommy are the North of England Champions. I was in a daze and even more so when I saw all of the other riders shaking hands with and congratulating Harry. I remember Curly rubbing his hand through my hair and congratulating me saying, "Well done lad." I was stunned the amount of congratulations I got and I was only this little twelve-year-old groom. As Harry rode out of the ring, I do not believe that anyone on the planet could have looked happier and as we were waiting for the presentation in this daze, his parents arrived from the member's pavilion.

CB

Mrs. Priestley was crying and Mr. Priestley already had a cigarette in his hand for Tommy who was as excited as could be with all of this fuss around him. I remember how he snatched that cigarette and ate it, for some unknown reason, he liked them and always received one from Mr. Priestley when he saw him. Naturally, this was the most incredible day of my life and I knew that nobody at home would believe me, but I didn't care, the truth was the truth and I was living it!

The show officials brought a table into the arena with a tablecloth, flowers and sitting right in the middle reflecting the afternoon sun was the beautiful large silver North of England Championship trophy that would be presented to Harry and Tommy. Once Curly got the word, all the horses that had been in the jump off, rode into the arena for their awards headed by Harry and Tommy to thunderous applause from the crowd.

Mr. Milton turned on his microphone and introduced all the dignitaries, sponsors and officials thanked the enormous crowd for coming out and supporting the Show Jumping that afternoon and then he got ready for the big awards. Presenting the trophy that day was Mr.

Robert Hanson from Yorkshire, one of the biggest officials and owners of top horses in the country. He was from Huddersfield and was the owner of a large haulage company, he owned Flanagan that Pat Smythe rode and O'Malley the mount of Harvey Smith. I will never forget how proud I felt when Mr. Milton said, "My Lords, Ladies and Gentlemen, the North of England Champion, from Southport, Lancashire, Mr. Harry Priestley riding Caruso." The crowd starting cheering and applauding again and Tommy loved every minute of it, he knew that he was the champion. He received the most beautiful sash that was put around his neck and a gorgeous championship rosette.

Once all of the awards and rosettes had been given out, Harry and Tommy led the victory gallop around the enormous arena to loud cheers from the crowd, what a finish to an amazing day.

As Harry rode through the entrance to the arena, he jumped off Tommy and threw me on top to ride him back to the horsebox. There were some of the Manchester reporters there waiting to talk to Harry, this was not important to me, I was sitting on the back of the North of England Champion, Caruso! I always remember Blossom, Harvey Smiths' groom congratulating me and telling me that one never grows tired of being a winner. I remembered her saying that and took it through life with me, this gave me a competitive edge and since then, I have always wanted to be the best at what I do and win! On the way back to the horsebox, so many of the watching public reached out and touched Tommy as we rode by and kept saying well done to me.

CS

I didn't quite understand it at the time, as it was Harry that rode Tommy to the win, not me but it sure made me feel good. Even when I got back to the horsebox and started to take Tommy's tack off, people still gathered and kept asking if they could stroke him. Some of the children told me how lucky I was to be the groom to a champion and some asked me how still only being a school had I achieved this? I was a little shy and just smiled back at most of them busying myself enough not to seem rude. They were right. I even asked myself if this was real and how had I managed to become part of this amazing sport of Show Jumping and its stars so young. I had though, through a little bit of nerve and persistence by asking the Priestleys if I could look after their horses. Little did I realize on that day where this sport would take me and how it would impact my life in the world of the horse?

Chapter Nine

After Harry had finished with the press, he and Doreen headed back to the horsebox and I had already prepared Tommy for the journey home and loaded him on board. I was standing there talking with him and hugging away when they both arrived. I don't think I had ever seen Harry so happy and he came up and gave Tommy some real pats on the neck and a little affection I had not seen before. Doreen of course was over the moon and decided after some fuss to make us a cup of tea and some of her delicious sandwiches before we set off on our journey home. I was wearing the big Red Rosette that Tommy had won on my jacket, they give red for first in the U.K. and the championship sash had pride of honor draped across the window of the horsebox. I was far too excited to eat, however, Doreen insisted I had a sandwich and the tea was delicious.

There were still some show jumping fans milling around and taking pictures of Tommy from the bottom of the ramp, which was a wonderful tribute to him. He did not seem to care and just kept munching away on his hay and occasionally laying back his ears and sent an occasional nip in Stars' direction. Tommy was always the boss and often let Star know that he was the elder and demanded respect, especially today as he was the North of England Champion.

ᑿ

Doreen cleared up all our afternoon tea leftovers and soon it was time to leave the show ground and make our way home, I did not want to leave. Harry said, "Don't worry; we will be at another big three-day show in a couple of weeks, the Liverpool Show." I wondered how many of the riders who were there today would be in Liverpool, I was not to be disappointed.

As we drove down the East Lancashire Road on the way home I remember sitting back in my seat, closing my eyes and dreaming about the day I would be the rider and receiving the big trophy while I rode

59

the victory gallop around the arena. Harry let me hold the beautiful silver trophy he had won that day and I cradled it all the way home. I wanted to keep it but it belonged to Harry and would take pride of place amongst his other trophies in the beautiful display case he had at his house. Pretty soon we pulled into the farmyard and the sun was setting with beautiful colors in the sky and I can remember what a scene it must have been as I led Tommy down the ramp into his stable. Doreen brought Star and we got them ready for the night by taking off their travel wraps, blankets and halters. I had already bedded their stalls down before we left in the morning so all that we had left to do was fill the water buckets, the hay nets and their well-deserved feed.

⚃

Doreen gave me a big hug and thanked me for everything, Harry said goodnight, they both climbed into his car and off they drove with that beautiful trophy. I walked back into Tommy's stall, being the only person he allowed in with him while he ate. I sat down in the straw and looked at my hero, so proud of him and he really knew how much I loved him. We had great trust in each other and I am convinced he would have let me sleep right there beside him for the night. Of course, while he was eating, he did not even acknowledge I was in there with him though he occasionally gave me a side-glance. I never remember him laying his ears back nor shaking his head at me, although it has to be said, when Tommy was eating, Harry couldn't get near him. Eventually, I decided to get on my bicycle and head home before it got dark and as I rode home I really believed that everyone I passed knew that I was the groom to the North of England Champion.

Nobody really cared, nor did they know but I was happy in my thoughts and that was all that mattered to me. I remember walking into the house and my parents sitting watching television, they had no interest whatsoever in my involvement with the horses that meant so much to me and even when I told them that Tommy had won that day, they did not seem to share the joy I had. It didn't really matter, I said goodnight and climbed the stairs to bed knowing it would be difficult to sleep that night. I did sleep and all of my dreams were of winning big show jumping events and representing Great Britain around the world and at the Olympics!

The next morning, Sunday, I headed back to the stables and as always I was greeted by wonderful neighs from my two friends. Mostly because they knew that any minute I was going to feed them, I don't know why, but Star's water was always filled with hay, so that had to be cleaned out and fresh water given to them both.

While they were eating, I brought the wheelbarrow around and mucked out their stalls throwing all the clean straw to the side. I remember how old fashioned the stalls were and underneath the straw was cobblestones. I always gave them a good sweep and once a week would put the two horses out to graze and hose down the floors. Today, Harry wanted them both to have the day off so this was a perfect time to turn them out. I took Tommy out first, let him go once I had closed the gate and he took off at high speed bucking and squealing as he galloped around the paddock. I waited a couple of minutes before I took Star out which gave Tommy a chance to settle down then I took Star out. As soon as I let him go, both of them decided to have some play time together and off they set at high speed, bucking, rearing with their tails held high enjoying the wind under them as they raced side by side around the field.

They soon settled and in no time started to graze quietly side-by-side, I took this as a perfect opportunity to hose down their stalls. After I had laid the fresh straw and bedded them down, I unloaded the horsebox, cleaned the tack, put it in the tack room and prepared the horsebox for the next show.

⌣

This was two weeks away and I knew it would seem like an eternity to me but what could I do? When all the work was done, I left the horses grazing and rode my bicycle down to the Priestley's house. I always walked through the big black gate leading to the back of the house and knocked on the door at the rear. It was always opened by Doreen and she was busy as usual, doing laundry, cleaning the kitchen having been upstairs already and made the beds. I was always greeted by her with a great smile, hugs and most of the time she called me by my nickname from her, Frankenstein; she still calls me that to this day.

I always thought she made the best coffee, boiling the milk in a pan and making it from scratch, I can still taste how good it was and never bitter, wonderfully creamy and sweet served often with the most delicious chocolate biscuits. Of course, we never stopped talking about the day before and Harry winning the North of England Championship. Late that afternoon, they had all decided to have a little party to celebrate and the family had all been invited which included me also. I had already met Joan, the youngest; she still lived at home and was a bundle of mischief with a wicked sense of humor. There were two other brothers whom I had not yet met, Derek and Jeffery. Derek, like Harry and Joan, also had a wicked sense of humor but what a wonderful family.

ఴ

I was to meet them all that afternoon at the party although I was a little shy, not to mention nervous, I had never been to a party like this before.

Doreen told me that she would come back to the stables with me and help get things finished and then come back to the house for the party and would love it if I helped her and Joan.

I left my bicycle at their house and off we set in her father's car, the beautiful Rover to the stables so that we could get the horses in and finish them for the day. I could not believe Tommy and Star, they had found some real wet patch of dark mud to roll in and it had by now dried all over their coats. Doreen held them while I hosed them off and brought out the sweat scraper to squeeze most of the water from their coats. It was also important that we dried their heels so they did not become cracked and spread a little Vaseline on them. Once we had finished and they were back in their stalls we fed them a little earlier than usual and Doreen told me that she would come back later and top up the hay nets.

We got back into the Rover and headed back to the house, we started to prepare everything for the celebratory party that was now planned for a six thirty start. They had a lovely dining room which overlooked a beautiful big garden and the back of the house faced direct west. There were French doors that opened to a lovely brick patio and not far from them were the sand dunes and the beach so we were fortunate to have magnificent sunsets.

ఴ

I spent quite some time helping Doreen in the kitchen and had a constant flow back and forth carrying plates and trays to the dining table. It was to be a buffet and my mouth was watering having never seen some of these incredible delicacies that Doreen was preparing for this feast. Harry was in the main lounge with his father, Mrs. Priestley and Joan was also helping us in the kitchen. Joan was amused by me and never stopped teasing which intensified when her brother Derek arrived, two peas in a pod we called them.

Jeff was the first to arrive and not long after came Derek, he immediately said, "This must be the Frankenstein that I've heard all about, how are ye lad?" He was actually very nice but they; Derek and Joan never stopped teasing and getting up to mischief. Mr. Priestley had poured drinks for everyone, I was far too young for alcohol, however they did make me a light shandy and we all sat outside on the terrace in the most beautiful late afternoon sun. The party was amazing; Mr. Priestley with everyone participating raised his glass and toasted a wonderful win to Harry from the day before telling him how proud he was of him. This was another world to me having come from a fairly humble background and was not used to this lavish socializing of the upper class.

ೞ

I have to admit though, they totally treated me like family and it was already being ensconced in my mind that this was the lifestyle I wanted.

At the party's end, I cycled home and it was never to be the same again, I knew now what I wanted and from that day forth decided I would go for it.

I had a wonderful four years with the Priestley family and during that first year I was with them, August arrived and one of the greatest shows in the country happened to be in our back yard. The Southport flower show was a three-day affair with top class show jumping every day and the evenings of the first two days incorporated jumping under the lights. The Southport show had a dream setting, right across the street from one of the longest, sandy beaches in the country. Next to the show ground was the Southport fair ground with everything you can imagine from the Ferris wheel to a big dipper, bumper cars, house of horrors and everything in between. Everybody came to Southport and even though it was only a three-day show, most people came for the week and made it a family holiday.

They all brought their caravans attached to the back of the horseboxes, the horses were stabled there and every day we rode out together on the beach, it was heaven. At night after the floodlit jumping many of the riders including myself would head off to the fair ground and we laughed the night away eventually getting back late and enjoying coffee in different caravans each evening.

ೞ

I had a battery operated record player then which I brought with me and we played 45's each night, Elvis, The Beatles, The Searchers, Cilla Black, Dusty Springfield, Gerry and the Pacemakers and many more. I can remember those nights as if it were yesterday and all of us had a blast telling jokes, talking show jumping and just drinking coffee. The teenagers in those days didn't even know what drugs were and life seemed so innocent to us all being very privileged to be a part of this amazing life on the circuit.

This was my first ever Southport Show and riders who would become legends in our sport were there, this was 1961 it was the first time I ever saw David Broome and Anneli Drummond-Hay live. I had seen them before on television but never in the flesh. Anneli had a magnificent horse called Merely-A-Monarch, I fell in love with him and both he and Anneli became two of my favorite show jumping combinations of all time. Ted Edgar was there from Warwickshire, John Bailey and Simon Rodgerson from Scotland, David Boston Barker and his brother William from Yorkshire, Graham Fletcher also from Yorkshire. Malcolm Pyrah who was riding for Trevor Banks from the Hull area, and Andrew Fielder with the unforgettable Vibart, also from Yorkshire. Of course, the great Harvey Smith was also there with a string of top horses including O'Malley, Harvester, Warpaint and The Sea Hawk, he also had a couple of young horses with him.

His groom Blossom was also taking care of Deric for Sammy Morphet and I offered to help her, as she appeared to really have her hands full. She discussed it with Harvey and he agreed, I was over the moon as at this show I only had Tommy. There were no Foxhunter classes for Star. In those days Harvey's mother was best friends with Sammy Morphet's mother and they seemed to go everywhere together. They both had walking sticks but loved the life of the show jumping circuit and always seemed to be there at the big shows. They both took a strong liking to me and made sure I was taken care of for the week while helping Blossom. At the end of the week, they both gave me a half a crown, which was two shillings and sixpence, combined, I had five shillings. I noticed on both of the half-crowns that they were dated 1948, the year I was born, five shillings in those days was a lot of money to a young boy but I could not spend them.

I felt I had been given the world, especially as one of them had been given to me by the mother of Harvey Smith, I still have those two half-crowns today and they are two of my most treasured possessions. Mrs. Smith and Mrs. Morphet are long gone now, I wonder what they would think if they were alive and found out I still have them, I must let Harvey know!

Each year in the early sixties, the Southport Show always held a large dinner dance for the competitors; at one of the big hotels.

&

That particular week, we all decided to go and Harry bought me a ticket. Not long before that dinner dance I had acquired my first ever grown up suit; with long trousers and dressed up for the evening, everyone was quite amused when they saw me in my suit with shirt and tie. When we were seated at our table, I noticed across the ballroom, Anneli Drummond-Hay, David Broome and Harvey Smith sitting at the same table.

After we had eaten dinner, I told Harry that I would love to dance with Anneli, he laughed and said, "Why don't you go and ask her." I thought, why not, got up from my chair and he thought it was hilarious but I headed for her table anyway. I remember it as if it were yesterday, I politely looked at her, she smiled, Harvey said, "Ow are ye lad" in his Yorkshire accent and I said, "Miss Drummond-Hay, would you please dance with me." I was expecting her to laugh but she graciously took my hand, smiled and said, "I would be delighted young man." My knees almost turned to jelly, we headed for the dance floor and I absolutely could not believe that I was dancing with one of the most famous show jumping riders of all time, Anneli Drummond-Hay. I was in such awe, I don't remember hearing the music, the noise of all the patrons or the hustle and bustle of that evening, it was just Anneli and I on the dance floor.

&

When the dance finished, I led her back to her table, thanked her, she thanked me and I headed back to my own table beside Harry, I never lived that night down. From that day to this, I have had a crush on Anneli and throughout her career until she left England for South Africa I was her number one fan. At one time, I even wanted to change my name to Drummond-Hay and swore that if I ever owned my own horse it would be called Merely-A-Monarch. As I got older and eventually became a rider, then a commentator, she and I became friends.

I have never forgotten that first ever Southport show and the wonderful time I had there. I remember one night being in Ken and Stephen Pritchard's caravan with quite a few of the show jumpers playing our records and Harvey popping his head in the door looking at me and telling me I should be in bed; it was after one o'clock in the morning.

I was always amazed how often when I was growing up that he did things like this and I never realized at the time how he was looking out for me. He really did seem to care and underneath his hard exterior was a wonderful caring man with a big heart. On the Thursday evening, I sat with his mother and Mrs. Morphet watching the jumping under lights, we always called it the floodlit jumping. I remember the evening opening up with a junior jumper class; it was called the 13.2" championship.

ᘓ

The ponies in those days were amazing, jumping around four feet courses and higher, the standard was incredible, but not unusual. It was a pretty big class and I remember David Bowen who at that time rode for Brian Dickson from Parbold, Lancashire riding this amazing little pony called Luck Money. He jumped an amazing clear round with several others and eventually came back for the jump off, wow, did they go around that course at break neck speed, jumped clear again and won the class.

Everyone around the arena and in the stands was on their feet, it was so exciting and David at the time could not have been more than twelve or thirteen years old. The standard amongst the pony jumpers was amazing with top riders from all over England. Lynn Raper was there with Keewis and Pierrot, two ponies that rarely ever had a fence down, in fact, she had won the Junior European Championship on Pierrot. She also held the title of leading junior Show Jumper of the year at the Horse of the Year Show and the leading Junior Show Jumper at the Royal International Horse Show. Many riders when they saw Lynn with her two ponies often said, "If Lynn is here, we might as well go home."

ᘓ

At that time, there was another young lady down in the south of England riding another 14.2" pony, few people had heard of her yet, until about three years later when she broke on to the senior circuit with that same pony, she was called Marion Coakes and her pony was Stroller, that is another story which will be told later on.

After the junior jumping was over it was time for the big two classes of the night, the first being a speed class which is a first round against the clock. Some of the best horses in Britain competed but when Harvey was there with The Sea Hawk, nobody ever stood a chance. He could do things with this horse that was impossible to anyone else and he did it again that night. The crowd was on the edge of their seats as Harvey rode Sea Hawk around the course at break neck speed. The twist and turns were unbelievable even turning at great angles in the air, he would land from one fence and would be over the other with ease in just two strides. Never in the history of show jumping had anyone seen a combination like Harvey and The Sea Hawk. Of course they won in record time and not one horse and rider in that class could come even close to catching them.

After the speed class was over, the main Grand Prix started with all of the top riders bringing out their best horses including Anneli with Merely-A-Monarch, David Broome with Ballan Silver Knight, Harvey with O'Malley and many other of our top riders including Malcolm Pyrah with Trevor Bank's Mister Whippy.

മ

It was an amazing class with several clear rounds and eventually in the second jump off it was David, Anneli, Harvey, Jean Goodwin, John Bailey and Malcolm. Of course, it was even more exciting as an almost record check for two hundred and fifty pounds was going to the winner, a fortune for a show jumping class in those days. From what I remember, most of the horses jumped clear but none could touch Malcolm riding Mister Whippy and he came out as the big winner that night. Trevor Banks was ecstatic and Malcolm was more excited than I had ever seen him before.

The victory gallop and the atmosphere that night under the outdoor lights was amazing, Trevor threw a big celebration after the arena had closed down for the night. Of course, Curly Beard was his usual self at the gate and being the life and soul of the party was on his way to celebrate with Trevor and the rest of the show jumping crowd. I so wanted to go but was too young to be in the big party marquee that was serving alcohol so I headed to one of the caravans and we played records and drank our coffee. It was still fun and we created our own party and I was just delighted to be part of it all. As I climbed into my bed, which was in the horsebox, a mattress above the cab, once again I dreamt of one day being the next Malcolm Pyrah and taking that victory gallop around the arena after receiving the winner's trophy in a major show jumping Grand Prix.

Chapter Ten

We had an incredible fun week at the Southport show that week and I made more friends and was becoming one of the crowd; being known now by quite a lot of the grooms and riders. Those I did not know soon became friends through introduction from others and it was starting to become second nature that I was involved in quite a few of the social activities involved on the circuit. The week after the Southport show we headed to Woolton, a picturesque area of Liverpool for the Woolton show. Sammy Morphet actually lived in Woolton and was a big wholesale and retail butcher in the area. Show jumping was his hobby and he seemed to get about a lot to the big shows with his grand prix horse, Deric. Sammy was quite a celebrity locally and lots of people came out to watch him compete.

It was always wonderful seeing his mother, a woman I will never forget and whenever Harvey Smith was around, so was his mother arm in arm with Mrs. Morphet sitting in the stands watching the jumping. They were definitely two of the characters of our sport and were well known and loved by all the riders and grooms. At Southport, the week before I had met Charlie Nuttall who was the Young Riders Champion of Great Britain with a big grey horse called Cambusito. Charlie was about sixteen and had a couple of novice horses also, Napier and Oro.

ଔ

He lived with his family in a lovely village in Lancashire called Withnell and their house, which was absolutely beautiful, was known as "The White House." It was located very close to the Lancashire moors with miles up on miles of riding with hills covered in heather and in those days one hardly saw another human being.

There was lots of livestock around including cattle and sheep which were kept in their grazing area within old stone walls, very much a part of the history of this unique area. A very big influence of Roman times included old derelict buildings built of local stone, ruins, old churches and a true look of history surrounded the area. My first job after leaving school would be with Charlie and his family with his mother Eileen, an amazing character on the circuit but this was still in the future and I did not know this at the time.

The Woolton show was really a wonderful day out for many people including local riders with their horses and being in early September, there was already the look of autumn. Some of the leaves had started changing and early morning there was often mist and fog around with the evenings drawing in now getting dark quite a bit earlier. We were only a month away from the Horse of the Year Show down in London, little did I know that this would be my first trip down there. Looking back, Tommy did pretty well and I remember Star jumping a clear there in the grade C class and they both brought ribbons home from Woolton.

∞

There were not many shows left in the area as in those days, September was really the close of the outdoor season and the ultimate show in Europe was coming up during the first week of October. I was more determined than ever to be there and did not know how I was to get there, nor where I would stay when I did arrive. At that time, my father worked for British Railways and was able to get free tickets so he got one for me to travel down to Wembley. Before this amazing journey in my life, we still had to rough Tommy and Star off for the winter and turn them out on a daily basis. Their winter coats were starting to come through and there really was no riding left now. By the third week of September, they were both ready to be left out overnight and it was a sad time for me knowing that the British Show Jumping season had come to an end.

The only consolation I had was knowing that I would go down to the Horse of the Year Show and this was the foremost thing on my mind. Of course, I still wanted to go down to the stables every day and take care of my two closest friends in the world, Tommy and Star. Apart from my trip to Wembley, I did this, every day even through the depths of winter with snow, ice, rain and bitter cold but I did not care.

Suddenly it was Friday, two days before I left on my journey for the Horse of the Year Show and I could not sleep.

∞

I had only ever seen it on television and now I was going to be part of the most incredible indoor show in the world, little did I know how unbelievable this experience would be. My suitcase was already packed and I had not told a soul in the Show Jumping world that I was going. I remember it as if it were yesterday heading for the station in Formby to take the train for Liverpool. In those days, trains from Southport stopped at Formby and ended their journey at Liverpool Exchange Station.

Once I arrived in Liverpool I had to walk across the city to Lime Street Station which was enormous to me having only travelled through there once when I was much younger. My parents had taken my two brothers and I down to London for the weekend and I was about to take the same midnight train. In those days the trains were all steam and it took more than six hours through the night to get down to London Euston. I remember the enormous steam engine at the front of the train and one can never forget that smell from the steam. The carriages had long narrow corridors with little cubicles off the corridor and each cubicle had a sliding door with blinds one could pull down, it was a wonderful way of travelling. That night I remember there was only myself and a gentleman in our carriage so we were able to lie down on the long seat, one on each side of the cubicle giving us one each however, I was far too excited to sleep.

❧

I remember it was an express train with only three stops on its way down to London, Edge Hill, Crewe and Watford Junction then Euston Station in London. I recall all of the sounds and sites of that journey as this enormous steam engine picked up speed and raced toward Great Britain's capital. The clickity click of the big wheels on the tracks, the constant toot from the driver of the big steam horn, the flashing lights of towns and villages as we raced through, it was wonderful and very exciting for a young boy. Eventually, the train pulled into this enormous station known as London Euston, one of three major railway stations in London, the other three being Kings Cross, Waterloo and Paddington. I got off and remember asking one of the British Rail Porters how to get to Wembley, my free ticket was destined for there and it was a short train ride from the center of London. On my arrival at Wembley railway station I was almost bursting with anticipation and still had to walk to the Empire Pool, the home of the Horse of the Year Show.

Just the thought of getting off the train at Wembley was exciting in itself as many of the Show Jumping world often just referred to the Horse of the Year Show as Wembley! I again asked a porter how to get to the Empire Pool, he gave me pretty straightforward directions and I proceeded to walk through the drizzle and suddenly, there it was in front of me. First thing one saw in those days were the enormous towers of the famous Wembley Football stadium but that did not interest me.

಄

Right there in front of me was the outside collecting ring with several riders schooling their horses and I was surprised to see the footing as almost black cinders. I was in awe to see different flags from various nations on the jacket pockets of the riders. Of course, this was the first time I would see many of the British riders from the south of England and there were many from south of London who had represented Britain in Nations Cups.

Douglas Bunn the founder of Hickstead, George Hobbs, Fred Welch, Sue Cohen, Dawn Palethorpe, Julie Nash, Alan Oliver, David Broome, Anne Townsend, Anneli Drummond-Hay and of course, the great Pat Smythe. This was just to name a few and then there were riders from all over Europe, Ireland, Germany, Holland, Belgium, France, Denmark, Norway, Sweden, Italy, even South Africa and the United States of America. I just stood in the drizzle not even feeling it in total awe at what I was seeing in front of me, the greatest riders in the world and I was right there with them. I still had no idea where my accommodation was going to be and headed indoors to the great Empire Pool, the home of the Horse of the Year Show. Even though it was morning, the atmosphere was nothing like I had ever experienced and I could not believe the amazing lights which of course made the colored show jumps stand out like you would not believe.

಄

I was somehow standing in a magical wonderland of the horse.

Then I heard this voice, I had never heard announcing like this before and I recognized it as the voice I had only heard on television as that of Dorian Williams. He was the voice of the Horse of the Year Show and also of the B.B.C., a voice I could have listened to forever. Little did I know at that time what an influence and mentor he would become to me in later years. The trust and honesty in those days one never gave a thought to, so I just walked in to the First Aid room which was run by the St. John Ambulance Brigade and asked this young man if I could leave my suitcase in here. He sort of looked puzzled but said it would be fine and we slid it under one of the stretchers and he asked me why I was walking around with a suitcase. I told him that I had come down from Lancashire over night to see the Horse of the Year show and had nowhere to stay. He could not believe it as I had travelled two hundred and fifty miles so he spoke to his superior and they agreed that I could sleep on one of the stretchers in the First Aid room.

I thought nothing of it and thanked them and the young man took me to have a bracelet fitted allowing me to be in that area which of course was also the area all of the riders gathered for competition. I still have that bracelet today as one of my prized possessions and at the time did not realize how important it was, nor how lucky I was to have it because it allowed me in quite a few restricted areas where the public could not go.

CS

Of course, one of those areas was the indoor collecting ring and the reserved seating area for the riders and grooms. The St. Johns Ambulance Brigade guys also got me some meal tickets and really were wonderful taking care of me during my time at Wembley. This would not happen today and it became a once in a lifetime experience. I saw quite a few riders from the north several times including Harvey and not one of them knew that I was sleeping in the First Aid room.

I am sure they all thought I was staying with one or the other and never questioned me as to whom. There were showers and wash facilities for all of the grooms and riders so I never gave anything a thought and enjoyed every minute of it. After I had settled and had some food the adventures of this never to be forgotten week were about to begin, and what a week it turned out to be. I never believed that fairy tales can come true, but they can, and they did.

Chapter Eleven

After showering and changing, I decided to head for the arena and watch some of the show jumping. As I entered the tunnel, which led to the arena, I could not believe who was standing by the entrance right in front of me, the men's world and Olympic Champion, Hans Gunter Winkler.

At that time, he was one of the most famous show jumping riders in the world and to hold both titles at the same time was amazing. I had only read about this man and seen him on television, I was in awe and slowly walked toward him, he had his back to me and as a twelve-year-old boy I was nervous and incredibly shy. I stood right next to him looking over the gate into this incredible floodlit arena watching a horse jump the course; the atmosphere was incredible, I was at Wembley, the home of the Horse of the Year Show. I kept looking at Hans Winkler, I don't know what made me do it but I reached out quickly and touched his arm. He looked around and saw me standing there, rubbed his hand through my hair and spoke to me. I could not believe that the greatest show jumper alive was speaking to me. He was pleasant, asked me my name and if I was riding at the show, I still cannot remember how I answered him and he smiled and walked back through the tunnel to the collecting ring.

CS

I just stood there taking it in and could not believe what just happened, I had touched, spoken to and had my head rubbed by Hans Gunter Winkler. I do not think I washed my hair for a week and told everybody that I had met him. It was one of the biggest thrills of my life.

There were two gates that opened into the arena and in those days the Junior Leaders Regiment cadets acted as the arena party and they were amazing. Two of them operated a gate each and opened them as each horse came in and out of the arena. I was amazed to see that the collecting ring steward was Curly and I think he was surprised to see me there. It was nice to spend a little time with him and listen to all of the famous names from around the world being called by him to go into the arena. I drank it in like you would not believe and thought it amazing that some of these riders smiled toward me as they entered the big arena.

Of course, where Curly was located, one could not see the arena because as each horse rode in two large curtains closed blocking our view. This was so the crowd could not see through to the collecting ring. However, I knew that there would be plenty of show jumping for me to watch, little did I know what other amazing equestrian events would be seen that week including some incredible displays of riding, personalities, heavy horses, pony club events, driving and of course, the incredible closing ceremony called the cavalcade with the tribute to the horse.

❧

This made me realize why it is called "The Horse of the Year Show" as it included everything that was related to the horse, it was not just show jumping, which at that time, was all that I had really experienced. Curly eventually told me to go and watch some of the show jumping, I think I was sort of in his way, though he knew that it was all new to me and that I was star struck which kind of amused him, however, he did have a job to do!

His daughter Carol was riding here with quite a few other riders from the north of England, many of whom I knew by then and he had hopes of Carol with Mayfly winning at least one of the big competitions. Anyone who wins at the Horse of the Year Show has a very important part to write on their resume and it goes down in the history of show jumping. I walked back through the curtains and this time into the seating area which was reserved for riders, officials, grooms and owners, the bracelet I was wearing was my pass into this very select corner of the seating. This amazing indoor arena was officially known as the Empire Pool and hosted many world-class events though to me, it was only the Horse of the Year Show that mattered and I was there. I picked a corner and just sat watching taking it all in and was fascinated at the incredible voice that was announcing all the horses and riders.

He told a little about each one and then announced the country they were representing and there was often a cheer from the crowd when one of the very famous British riders entered the arena.

ೞ

There was something about his voice that captured my inner being, I did not know what it was then and never dreamt that later in life he would play such a part in my commentary career and become a good friend, his name was Dorian Williams, the voice of show jumping, Olympic games, European Championships and B.B.C. Television. A few days from now I would not just be drawn in to his voice, but his amazing delivery for the Cavalcade and the closing ceremony, I have never forgotten that night, nor will I ever. I watched a couple of classes and then another announcer took over from Dorian and I was disappointed not to be listening to his velvety voice anymore. It was fascinating to watch Alan Ball building the courses and to the riders from all over the world coming in to walk and pace the course before riding it.

For the evening performance I was back in the select little area of seating for the competitors and tonight, Monday was to be the Butlin Championships. At that time in show Jumping Butlin Holiday Camps were a big sponsor and held qualifying events throughout the year at their holiday camps. These qualifying rounds all led to the finals at the Horse of the Year Show and it was an enormous evening for them including the riders whom had qualified.

ೞ

Many of the Butlin Redcoats were brought in by coach and acted as ushers in the stands for the public who bought tickets; of course, it was always a sell out! Sir Billy Butlin the owner and founder was always there to present the trophy's and his box was always full of family, shareholders and V.I.P.'s.

All of the top riders from Great Britain and Europe competed in these classes and from what I remember; the foreign riders were invited to compete in the Butlin Championships.

This was my first time ever at an evening event at the Horse of the Year Show and the atmosphere was electrifying. More than eighteen thousand people filled the stands and like myself, all of them looked forward to a tremendous evening of world class Show Jumping. We were not to be disappointed with riders competing from more than fourteen nations, all wanting the coveted Butlin Championship and prize money. There were two major classes that night; one speed event and the main championship jumped over three rounds. I remember the tremendous excitement from the crowd as each horse and rider rode the speed course, some really fast and others a little slower. Some had fences down others jumped great clear rounds, then Harvey Smith came in aboard 'The Sea Hawk', I still believe him to be the greatest speed horse of all time.

 C3

A little grey that could turn on a sixpence and as soon as the bell was rang, off they set around the course and Harvey twisted and turned like you would not believe.

He even turned in mid-air and Seahawk came home clear knocking seconds of every other horse, he held that lead until the end, no other horse could catch him and he was crowned the winner of the first major competition of the show. The audience gave an enormous cheer as Harvey led in the recipients for their awards, he was not only incredibly popular, Harvey won the competition for his host nation, Great Britain. Before the main class of the night, we were treated to the musical drive of the heavy horses, the horse personalities, the pony club mounted games, always brought the crowd to their feet cheering on their young teams and a wonderful display from the Spanish Riding School of Vienna.

The beautiful jumps were set and it was time for the riders to walk the course for the Butlin Championship. The course had been designed by Alan Ball and the Junior Leaders Regiment under his supervision had all of the jumps in place looking spectacular.

The gates at the entrance to the arena opened and in came all the riders in their finery, their polished boots, white britches and beautiful red jackets which in England we called Hunting Pink.

C3

Many of the jackets had the flag of the nation each rider was representing sewn into the flap of their top pocket. To me, there was nothing more magical than this incredible site I was witnessing for the first time. From where I was sitting, the course looked enormous and I only wished that I was one of the riders out there showing my skills to this enormous crowd and the millions that would be watching on B.B.C. Television. As I sat watching the course walk, as always, my thoughts were dreaming of what I hoped one day would be. Me out there in this magnificent arena walking the course with all of these world class riders and beating them all against the clock bringing the crowd to its feet as the National Anthem of Great Britain was played after my award ceremony.

Suddenly the bell was wrung indicating the end of the course walk. The riders headed out to their grooms who were waiting with their top International horses so they could warm them up and start the competition. The great Dorian Williams was commentating that night and once again I was drawn in to his magnificent voice as he told the crowd all about the sponsor, Butlins. He also talked about how many nations were represented that night and then talked a little about the course and how it would all be judged under the rules of the F.E.I.

ՏՑ

If you are not familiar with the F.E.I., it is the governing body of International equestrian competition known as the Federation Equestriane Internationale based in Geneva. When Dorian had finished, another commentator took over the arena announcing as Dorian put on his other announcing hat and became the commentator for B.B.C. Television.

I was disappointed that he would not be announcing that night, however, it turned out that Dorian would always cover the B.B.C. Commentary and only when they were not covering an event would Dorian announce in the arena.

The Butlin Championship was full of excitement with riders going clear in the first round from several nations including Great Britain. Naturally, every time a British rider rode a clear round the cheers were much higher and the applause was much louder. The British though were always fair to the riders from overseas always giving them a wonderful reception and treated them with great respect when they rode clear or won. I was enthralled with it all and had never experienced anything like it and how I wished that Tommy was here competing. He was not an international horse and did not qualify for the Horse of the Year Show, a great disappointment to me.

ՏՑ

As the evening drew on, the first jump off was under way and all of the horses and riders that had gone clear came back for the next round. Obviously, there was a time allowed but this particular round was not against the clock, this was to be the second round and boy did that turn out special. In this first jump off from what I remember, about six or seven horses jumped clear again and headed to the final round, the jump off against the clock. Harvey was one of them including David Boston Barker from Northallerton in Yorkshire and what a jump off it turned out to be. Each horse and rider brought the crowd to its feet and the eventual winner was David Boston Barker riding Lucky Sam. The Butlin Championship stayed in Great Britain and the crowd was elated with a home win. When it was all over everybody headed down to the stabling area, there were celebrations, parties, coffee served in various caravans and fun was had by all, it was absolutely for me, another spectacular night to remember.

I drank hot Ovaltine and ate Ovaltine biscuits with my friend Hazel who was now grooming for Harvey Smith, Hazel and I spent a lot of time at the Ovaltine caravan. We are still great friends and keep in touch, she has a livery stable and horse feed company with her husband Tom in Calverley near Leeds in Yorkshire.

ℛ

Ovaltine was one of the main sponsors and on Wednesday night they would sponsor the Leading Show Jumper of the Year, I could not wait to see that class. Eventually, I headed back to the first aid room, curled up on my stretcher and soon fell asleep which was amazing considering how exciting I felt.

Chapter Twelve

The next day, Tuesday started off with the final of the Daily Express Foxhunter Championship, this was the ultimate for young horses to have qualified for Wembley.

Many unknown riders and also top international riders had qualified their young horses for this competition and it was known that often the winner would go on to be a top class show jumper. As always; it was a very exciting event and very prestigious indeed. Of course, every rider wanted to win this coveted trophy for young horses. Some had already reached Grade A, which in England was the Grand Prix level so the competition was close and hot. From what I remember, it was won that year by Althea Roger Smith riding Rockwell who went on to become one of our top international lady riders. As the previous night had been gala night, Tuesday was the official opening of the Horse of the Year Show and it was so exciting. As the day went on, I saw the Prince Phillip Cup which was the Pony Club mounted games, so much fun with teams from all over England, Wales and Scotland and the pace was incredible.

Naturally, in London there were people from all over United Kingdom who got behind their teams and the air was electric as they galloped at break neck speed up and down the arena.

慓

Sack races, relay, bending poles, cones, you name any athletic event and they did it on the backs of their ponies, and boy did they take every risk possible, it sure gave the competition amazing excitement. Each day points were gained; teams eliminated all building up to the Championship at the weekend, which I was looking forward too very much! Tuesday was also the day of several other competitions including the Newcomers Trial Stakes, The Overture Stakes and the big class of the evening, an international competition, The Philips Electrical Championship.

On Wednesday, it was an enormous day for all the Show Jumpers with lots of competitions including the Dick Turpin Stakes, the Gordon Richards Stakes, The Guinness Time Championship and the Show Hunter of the Year.

The main event of the evening was the Ovaltine Championship known as the Leading Show Jumper of the Year competition and I had friends competing including Andrew Fielder with his great horse Vibart. There was a top International field from all over Europe and Andrew was the youngest in the competition at only sixteen years of age. He was one of the first round clears and his father Jack was as excited as anyone in the building that night. The jump off was amazing, Andrew was the last to go and with the tension so intense everyone had goose bumps.

CB

It was always exciting when Vibart came into the arena as I have mentioned, he was known for his famous kick back which he did at every jump bringing gasps and laughs from the audience. You can imagine what this was like with close to eighteen thousand in the arena that night. The bell was wrung and the combination of Andrew and Vibart set off around the course.

Half way around what was the final round against the clock, Andrew was clear, suddenly, there were only two fences to go and they were still clear and fast. I can clearly remember Jack, Andrew's father standing next to me and he could hardly contain himself and as Andrew and Vibart came through the finish, Jack looked up at the clock, saw the time, picked me up and through me in the air shouting, "He has done it, I can't believe it, he has done it." The crowd was absolutely on the edge of its seats and the cheering was unbelievable, Andrew appeared to be stunned. He came out with an enormous smile on his face and everyone was congratulating him, especially as he had just become the youngest in history to win this coveted title, Leading Show Jumper of the Year! What celebrations that night and everyone toasted Andrew as a young man who had just made show jumping history and I became a part of a night never to be forgotten.

CB

I believe (although I stand to be corrected) that record of the youngest ever to win the Leading Show Jumper of the Year still stands. Thursday brought us the London Stakes, Lonsdale Memorial Stakes and the Leading Junior Show Jumper of the Year. The main evening performance brought us the Evening News Cup followed by the Puissance with many of Europe's top horse's and rider's taking part, better known at the Horse of the Year Show as the night of the big wall! The one thing that amazed me was the small horse from Ireland Dundrum ridden by Tommy Wade as one of the entries for this competition. Dundrum only stood at 14. 3" and looked so small with a grown man in the saddle, nobody knew the size of the heart this little pony had as he was part of the distinguished field that night. From what I remember, the wall started off at about five feet six inches and always faced away from the entrance to the arena.

I was standing in the entrance, the two gates, and as horses came toward us on the other side of the wall, one could hardly even see the rider, let alone the horse. Dundrum and Tommy of course totally disappeared and could not be seen until they came over the wall which they did like a cat. He cleared the course including the wall three times much to the delight and excitement of a sold out house that night. He was now into the jump off with the wall standing at seven feet two inches with about three other horses and riders through to this fourth round jump off.

ᔆ

Tommy was the first to go and you could have heard a pin drop as they set off around the course. There were only two jumps that mattered, the big triple spread and the wall standing at seven feet two, which looked enormous standing in the middle of the arena. They jumped the practice fence and then came around to the big triple and had no problem with that and cantered down to the end of the arena.

As they made the turn toward the wall, we at the far end, lost sight of them, we did not know how close to the wall they were when there was an enormous gasp from the crowd. Suddenly, we saw these two little legs climbing over the wall, Dundrum's stomach caught a brick but it did not come down and they landed safely on the ground with the wall intact, the crowd rose to its feet cheering, clapping, banging their feet, whistling and Tommy took off his hat and through it high into the air. The atmosphere was electric and the other riders decided that they would not go and gave the first prize to the little pony with the heart of a lion. Tommy Wade and Dundrum, the combination from Ireland had won the Puissance that night in the most unbelievable style ever, it was purely a magical night for show jumping and certainly a week that was building full of memories for me.

GS

After the night before and this, being the first time I had ever seen a Puissance live, I could not believe that I was actually living this and was really there amongst all of this top international history in show jumping being made at Wembley.

Friday's competitions included the Daily Telegraph Cup, the William Hanson Trophy and the main competition of the day, an international competition, the Sunday Times Cup. There had been many other disciplines crowned that week including Romeo, the Hunter, Pollyanna, the Pony, Mirage, the Hack, all horses and ponies of the year in their particular discipline.

Back to the Show Jumping at the 1963 Horse of the Year Show, the great Anneli Drummond-Hay with her amazing horse Merely-A-Monarch won both the Guinness Time Championship and The Sunday Times Cup.

Olympian Peter Robeson won the Ronson Trophy, the Victor Ludorum riding Frecrest, his Olympic mount and Robert Woodward riding Sherree won the Pontin Trophy for the Young Rider of the Year Championship!

All of this was the lead in to the final night on Saturday when so many horses and riders would be introduced at the closing ceremony and cavalcade for the year 1963. Competitions included on this final day the Pontin Trophy, the Horse and Hound Stakes, Country Life and Riding Cup and the Ronson Trophy for the Victor Ludorum Championship, a major International Competition.

GS

What a night that was to include the crowning of the Prince Phillip Cup Winners for the Pony Club Mounted Games Championship, which was actually presented by His Royal Highness Prince Phillip. The team that came through and took top honors came from Scotland and the trophy was presented to the Angus branch of the Pony Club.

These boys and girls could not hold their excitement as they galloped around the most prestigious horse show arena in the world displaying their trophy to the equally excited crowd. They truly brought the Horse of the Year Crowd at Wembley to their feet and thoroughly deserved their end of year championship, the most coveted trophy in the whole of the British Isles Pony Club!

When all the competitions, displays and awards were given out on that final night, the Junior Leaders Regiment RAC, the Horse of the Year Show arena party cleared the course for the final time that year to make way for the Cavalcade. The excitement was electric both from the riders who would participate and from the crowd who had paid the highest prices of the week for tickets. Little did I know at that moment in time what an impression this would make on me and how it would influence my future as an announcer.

ᘓ

This moment in history had been rehearsed and rehearsed with unbelievable precision right down to the exact spot each horse and rider would stand, whether it be; as an individual or a team member. The Host, Master of Ceremonies for that night would be the Show Jumping voice of the B.B.C., and the Horse of the Year Show, Dorian Williams who would bring the house down as only he could.

Once everything was ready, the house lights were dimmed and several spotlights shone their bright beams toward the entrance of the arena and Dorian's voice announced, "Your Royal Highnesses, VIP's, Ladies and Gentlemen, Boys and Girls, the Cavalcade for 1963 is about to commence. The Band of the Royal Army Service Corps started to play the Overture and once the music came down in volume Dorian started to introduce the participants in the Cavalcade. Every single person, horse, winner and team that participated drew gasps and applause from the sold out crowd.

The horses and riders that had won major championships throughout the year including our National Champion's in all disciplines. There were all our international riders whom had represented Great Britain on various teams. Then we had the visiting riders from overseas including team members and those who had come to display as well as compete.

ᘓ

Grand National winners and all of the horses and participants in the Parade of Personalities, The Police Horse of the Year, The winners of the Pony Club Mounted Games, Prince Phillip Cup, The Heavy Horses, The Dressage and Event Horses of the Year, the winners of the Wembley and Harringay Spurs, the winners of every major class at this

Horse of the Year Show, The Horses of the Year, the Riders of the Year, Our Olympic Riders from every Discipline, the Quadrille of the Year, and much more than I can remember. Finally, Dorian announced to the waiting audience that the Cavalcade for 1963 was now assembled.

The band stopped playing, the audience hushed to almost silence, even the horses seemed to know something special was about to happen and I still did not know what was coming having never experienced this before. I was so wrapped up in this Cavalcade of unbelievable talent and fame that was in this arena my head was spinning. I was suddenly brought down to earth as Dorian's voice started to narrate "The Tribute to the Horse." *And where in this wide world can man find nobility without pride, friendship without envy or beauty without vanity. Here, where grace is laced with muscle and strength by gentleness confined. He serves, but without servility, he has fought, but with no enmity. There is nothing so powerful, yet nothing less violent. There is nothing so quick, yet nothing more patient. England's past has been born on his back, all of our history is his industry, we are his heirs, he our inheritance, The Horse!*

CB

During the narration of this; one could have heard a pin drop, even the horses seemed to remain silent, as Dorian finished and said, Ladies and Gentlemen, The Horse, the arena erupted with cheers and while looking around I could see that many hundreds of people were wiping tears from their eyes. The atmosphere was unbelievable, horses were now excited by the applause and everyone became a part of this magnificent spectacle and occasion. When everything calmed down, Dorian then acknowledged all whom had contributed in making the Horse of the Year Show the great success that it had been and everyone joined hands and sang Auld Lang Syne bringing this amazing week to a close and also the equestrian season for 1963. To everyone back in the stabling area it was extremely sad as we all knew that it was the long winter ahead with no more horse shows.

In those days, we did not have a winter circuit and it was only a handful of our top international riders and their grooms that travelled abroad in the winter.

Those of us who did not have this honor or luxury, were left extremely sad with the prospect of a long winter at home ahead.

Chapter Thirteen

That night none of us slept knowing that we would be leaving this magical place the next morning, I didn't even begin to think how sad I would feel as I walked away from the Empire Pool and the home of the Horse of the Year Show known to us all simply as Wembley! I remember walking through the indoor collecting ring to take one last look at the arena before I left.

It was not the same, full of bulldozers clearing the arena, all the officials were gone, no jumps or arena party and it seemed totally violated to all of us saying our farewells, it just was not the same and made us even sadder to be saying goodbye. The 1963 Show Jumping season was now at an end and our family of Show Jumping Gypsies were at a loss with us all hugging, and saying goodbye to each other. Many of the grooms whom had travelled with show jumpers were now joining the hunting yards for the winter and some became unemployed. Of course, I was still at school and knew that I had to go back on my return home and faced a long winter of looking after Tommy and Star with never leaving our immediate area. There would be no more shows and I knew that after this winter was over, I would have a choice of staying at school or joining one of the show jumping families and travelling full time around Europe.

ೞ

I left the Empire Pool and headed for Wembley station to catch a train to London Euston where I would connect with the train for home and I had never felt so heavy in my life. It was a grey day, drizzle was falling and the day had a feel of winter, our long sunny days had gone and all the leaves had started to fall from the trees. England is desolate in the winter and almost takes a ghostly look, tree limbs with no leaves, long days with only a few hours of daylight and seems like it will never end. In those days many homes still had coal fires and you could see lots of smoke coming from the chimneys of homes and industry climbing its way to the dark gray sky and I could see all of this from the train window as it headed north from London Euston to Liverpool. The journey was uneventful except for the sadness I was feeling after leaving such an amazing week at Wembley, I actually felt that everyone on the train was staring at me knowing I had been such a part of the Horse of The Year Show.

Of course, nobody knew who I was and much less cared but I felt amazingly important, as I knew that none of these people had just spent a week of their life with such excitement and famous equestrians. In those days all of the European and American show jumping riders were household names and I knew quite a lot of them, which at that early age gave me a feeling of importance.

ᙟ

I remember as the train approached Liverpool that I would soon see Tommy and Star again and this gave me a boost and took away some of the sad feelings. I knew even then that I would never forget my first experience at the Horse of the Year Show and I haven't. I still remember much of it as if it were yesterday.

After the train arrived in Liverpool Lime Street I walked across to Exchange station and took the local Southport train to Formby where I lived and remember arriving at the house.

Nobody seemed to bother that I was home and did not seem interested in hearing what an amazing week that I had just experienced at Wembley as a young man on my own. My family knew nothing of nor even had the slightest bit of interest in horses so there was no point in pursuing the issue. I went up to my room, unpacked the suitcase and settled in to the daily routine of once again being home and a part of the everyday reality of my family's life. In those days, we had no telephone so my contact with the Priestley's would not be until the following day and I was looking forward to riding to the stables on my bicycle and seeing my beloved horses and the family who had changed my life forever. The following day I was back at school and at the end of the day I headed for Woodvale and the stables and was greeted by neighing from my two friends, Tommy and Star. I did not realize how they had missed me and within in minutes, Harry arrived not knowing I was going to be there to feed.

ᙟ

87

I think he was pleased to see me knowing that the work would now be taken out of his hands. There was not a lot to do as the horses were now finished showing for the season and turned out during the day so apart from feeding that evening and mucking out the two stalls, there really was nothing to do. This was soon accomplished and I brought them both in from the field, let them into their stalls, gave them their evening feed and a net full of hay and left. Doreen worked during the day and did not get home from Liverpool until after six so I knew I would not see her until the following weekend and I set off home. On Saturday I did my job in reverse and headed down to the stables in the morning, fed, watered and turned the two horses out for the day. After all my chores were done I headed to the house and there was Doreen with the usual smile and her warm greeting.

She always made me coffee with hot milk and the usual milk chocolate biscuits; she couldn't wait to hear all my stories from the previous week at the Horse of the Year Show. I was in awe of course because she was a built in audience who genuinely wanted to know. I told her everything and more and being the wonderful person she is, Doreen shared in my excitement and constantly wished she had been with me, I wished she had too! Soon I left for home and as the long winter set in, the Horse of the Year show seemed like a dream now, as did my world of horse shows and the trips around the country with Doreen and Harry.

CB

I missed my evening rides on Tommy very much and knew that he would not be ridden now until at least March of the following year. I dreaded the long winter ahead and it seemed no time at all when I was leaving school and heading for the stables on my bicycle in very cold weather.

I was dedicated to my task and did this, every day seven days a week and do not remember missing a day. My four years with this amazing family changed me forever and led me on the path to a different way of life from the one I was raised. I distanced myself more and more from my real family and rarely spent much time there, except to sleep. Over the four-year period, we travelled to many shows and both horses had their share of ribbons, but we never repeated a major win like we did when Harry and Tommy became the North of England Champions in Manchester. Over that four-year period, I had become friends with many of the Show Jumpers and several were quite keen on giving me full time work when I left school. I decided I did not want to go to college but to work with my beloved horses during the day and further my education at night school.

Soon, my adventures into the full time world of Show Jumping was about to begin and I was also developing skills as a rider though at that time in my life I was content to just go out into that exciting world and become one of the many grooms who were so much a part of the backbone of our sport.

 C8

Little did I know what the future held and that one day I would be on the other side of the fence in official capacities and announcing some of the biggest shows and events in the world.

Chapter Fourteen

As the time passed toward leaving school, I grew more and more excited at the prospect of joining my amazing world of horses on a full time basis and could not wait until the day I was working and traveling full time in this magnificent sport. I had made friends with many of the riders during my time of traveling with Harry and Doreen.

Several of them had offered me work on leaving school. I knew that I would have to start as a groom and at that time of my life, I really didn't care if this would be a position held forever. Some of my best friends were grooms, to some of the most famous horses in the world and they had become a kind of celebrity themselves. One of my dear friends at the time and still is was Hazel who worked for Harvey Smith, I also knew Monica who was with David Broome and Merlin who worked for Anneli Drummond-Hay. I felt so privileged to know them and wanted to have a job working with one of them. It was not possible as they all had prime positions with nothing available in their yards at the time.

કૃ

I had a friend from the sport who had won the Young Riders Championship of Great Britain, called Charlie Nuttall and he offered me a job straight from leaving school.

I decided to leave school early and to continue my education at night school where I took "Office and Business Studies". I left school to join Charlie and his horses in March of 1964, I was fifteen years old. I could not be more excited knowing that I would be doing this now on a full time basis. I had already said my farewells to the Priestley family though I somehow knew that this would be a lifelong friendship. Here I am today still extremely friendly with Doreen, we talk on the phone, send each other Birthday and Christmas cards and remain close even to this day. I have so much to thank her for, she totally changed my life and put me on the path of this wonderful sport and my beloved horses.

I left school on a Tuesday evening and left my parent's house very early Wednesday morning taking the train with just one suitcase of belongings and started my adventure into this amazing world that I had created since the age of eleven.

If there had been 'A Lotto' in those days, you would have thought I had won it. The Nuttall family had an enormous home on several acres called the White House, it was so beautiful and Charlie's mother was an absolute character, her name was Eileen but I always called her Mrs. Nuttall.

ଔ

She was one of the most eccentric people I'd ever met in my life and was really Charlie's right arm when it came to the horses. She drove the horsebox and was animal crazy; it was not unusual to set off with a fox on a leash, two cats, a couple of parrots in their cages and FiFi the miniature poodle to a horse show. I believe that every time she drove that enormous horsebox out of her driveway, people were warned for miles around that she was on the road. Mrs. Nuttall or Mrs. Nut as we called her was a constant chain smoker and would often burst into a fit of coughing and I swear she totally stopped breathing.

When this happened, the horsebox shot from lane to lane, the parrots squawked, the fox howled, the cats meowed and FiFi barked her head off while Charles and I prayed out loud that she would not hit somebody. This was 1964. The poor horses in the back did everything in their power to stay balanced and stopped themselves from falling over. She would go blue in the face but somehow managed to get herself under control without either passing out of having a heart attack. Charlie was only four years older than I and was still not old enough to drive this enormous horsebox. It was rather fancy and was one of the nicest I had ever seen.

ଔ

The whole front of it was living quarters and the height of luxury. It was so beautiful; one could live in it.

However, that's merely an introduction there to Mrs. Nut and her zoo of animals that became part of the entourage that travelled to the shows, more of her later.

Charlie was a great guy and we had many laughs together and rode out a lot over the moors on Oro and Napier. I loved to ride Napier, he was an English thoroughbred and was one of the most beautiful rides I ever had. He was like riding a cloud, not to mention how gorgeous he was to look at. When Charlie rode Oro and I was on Napier, we often galloped across the moors we would jump stone walls, gates, hedges and each time we landed, it was like landing on a large marshmallow when I was aboard Napier. He was an amazing ride; I have never experienced a horse so comfortable as he. Charlie and I would get up each morning and head down the hill from the house to his stable block and his piggery. He was actually a breeder of pigs and had quite a famous business called "Cock of the North" Piggery's and was respected on a national basis. He had two boars, Sam and Nathaniel with many sows.

When every one of the sows had a litter, Mrs. Nut would get a big feed canister, rattle it and the mother with her babies, often twenty of them would follow her up to the house.

CB

They had a beautiful smoking room in Elizabethan style with a sit in fireplace and Mrs. Nut would lead them into that gorgeous room, allow the sow to lay out in front of the fire feeding her babies while Mrs. Nut sipped on very expensive scotch on the rocks. I do not believe I ever saw her without a cigarette in her mouth and the rest of the time she had a glass of whiskey in her hand. I never did know how she sipped her whiskey so elegantly with that cigarette dangling from her lips, she was one in a million, I loved her. She was a very kind woman and was good to me, except when it came to money, in those days I lived as family and was given one pound a week spending money with half a day off.

I did not care because I was doing what I loved with the horses.

When Charlie and I arrived down the hill each morning, he would go to the right to feed and muck out his pigs while I went to the left to take care of my horses. Once the mucking out and feeding was done we would head up to the house for a wonderful English breakfast. They had a housekeeper from Blackburn. Her name was Sandra who I think was secretly in love with Charlie, she took great care of us and was a wonderful young woman. Charlie and I would sit down at a large table in the most magnificent kitchen and be fed this wonderful breakfast cooked by Sandra.

CB

Mrs. Nut would pop in occasionally from the smoke room with the cigarette dangling, often wearing a sheepskin jacket with her nightdress under it after sitting up all night with her pigs. Many a time I would go to the bottom of the stairs to head up to my room and a couple of squealing baby pigs would come galloping out of the smoke room.

I learned to live with it after a while and nothing surprised me in that crazy house. It was fun though and Sandra and I had many a laugh over a cup of tea talking about the antics of Mrs. Nut. Charlie had a brother John who worked at the family company with his father in Bolton. A very successful engineering company that made them tons of money, they were in fact absolute millionaires. Charlie and John also had a sister who was a well-known violinist in Europe, her name was Jennifer but she did not come home much. She spent a lot of time travelling and playing the violin with all the top orchestras and conductors. Jennifer was very highly respected in the world of classical music. On the occasions she came home, Jennifer appeared nothing like the rest of the family and was an absolute sweetheart of a lady, I loved Jennifer.

Having joined the Nuttal's in March, it was about six weeks before we actually travelled to our first horse show, what an experience that was.

I was quite excited that morning as I got up much earlier to get Oro and 'Nappy' read for their first show that year.

◌ß

Nappy is what we called Napier for short and boy did he look gorgeous. He was a seven-year-old light bay thoroughbred and his coat shone like the feathers of a raven. Oro was a Chestnut, a pretty big horse with a big head but with the most beautiful, gentlest nature, he would not hurt a fly. I packed everything we would need for the show into the horsebox, saddles, bridles, grooming kits, hay nets, feed, hoof oil, buckets and everything that was needed. At last I loaded the two horses and after securing the ramp we were ready to leave. Charlie came down with his riding clothes, boots and crop and placed them in the wardrobe and here comes Mrs. Nut with the familiar cigarette hanging out of her mouth carrying FiFi the miniature poodle under her arm.

I don't believe I have ever seen more makeup on a lady and she had totally shaved off her eyebrows and a large thin black pencil line was drawn over each eye, I thought it was Joan Crawford. She wore a sheepskin Jacket I had not seen before, a lovely blouse, pair of slacks and suede shoes on her feet. She looked very smart, except for all the makeup and her hair looked like a mass of cotton balls stuck on the top of her head. I could not take my eyes off her and used the excuse of telling her how lovely she looked. Oh, by the way, her eyes were covered in thick green eye shadow that looked like a cars headlights.

ᘒ

The zoo had already been loaded and after a last minute check, off we rolled down the driveway toward the road. Charlie walked out into Chorley Road to guide his mother out and away we drove through the gates on the way to our first show of 1964.

We headed out of the village through Withnell and headed for the M6 Motorway. After entering this busy highway, Mrs. Nut started to cough, I really believed that day she was going to stop breathing all together and pass away right there at seventy miles an hour!

This by the way was my first experience of Mrs. Nuttall having a coughing fit while driving a very large horsebox full of animals, frightened the life out of me and everything else on board. I really did think everyone and everything in that horsebox was going to die that day. Like I experienced many times after that, she recovered and lived another day to drive that massive horsebox though I always travelled with her in total fear of my life and everything else on board. I really do believe at the age of fifteen, Mrs. Nut gave me my first grey hairs.

If that had been today with the amount of traffic on the roads, we surely would not have survived as she crossed three lanes of motorway several times with two parrot cages swinging back and forth, the horses trying to hold their footing in the back, cats meowing and both the dog and fox were cowered under my seat whimpering.

ᘒ

She of course, was totally oblivious to all of our fears and continued puffing at her cigarette through the whole fiasco as she became blue in the face. When things had settled down and she somehow managed to get oxygen into her lungs, we found a service station so that she could get out and head to the public toilet. I sat in the cab with the small zoo of animals and the horses in the back enjoying the safety and tranquility of a parked horsebox. Suddenly I saw her coming back toward us and all I could focus on was her Joan Crawford eyes covered in makeup and eyeliner.

She pulled herself into the cab, tuned on the ignition and we set off toward the motorway once again. As she pulled out of the car park onto the main slip road, there was a loud honking of horns from our right as an enormous articulated lorry that had the right of way was about to plough into our side. She was too busy lighting another cigarette to check the side mirror and give way, another moment of a near death experience. Don't ask me how, but somehow we all survived? Once on the M6 we headed south toward Birmingham as we were going to a show at Balsall Common in Warwickshire. It was a cold grey day and we arrived safely.

ଔଷ

Oh, I forgot to mention, on the back of the horsebox was a caravan, very nice one at that; this was Mrs. Nuttall's home from home. Charles and I slept in the living quarters of the horsebox while she lived in the caravan with her small zoo and cigarettes.

I am quite convinced that if I had lived in there with her I would have been dead of smoke inhalation within twenty-four hours. Having parked up, I let down the ramp and led the horses to their temporary stables. Oro was an old hand at this, but Napier being a little hot which was typical of thoroughbreds, was quite excited, tail in the air, neighing and snorting all the way to his stable, Oro never blinked an eyelid.

In the meantime, Mrs. Nuttall was preparing her caravan, Charles had wound down the supporting legs and she was going to cook us some food and put the kettle on for tea. I settled the horses down with fresh bedding; feed and full hay nets and filled their water buckets. This was the day before competition and we decided after the journey to leave the horses until the following morning before riding them.

After the horses were settled we headed to the caravan and Mrs. Nut was cooking something in a frying pan, I still cannot remember from that day to this what it was but Charles and I managed to eat it and boiled the kettle again to wash the dishes while mother enjoyed half a packet of cigarettes in about ten minutes.

ଔଷ

I am and always will be convinced that the dog, cat, parrots and fox all had lung cancer. Thank God Charles did not smoke because he and I shared the cab living quarters of the horsebox. That evening, he and I walked around the stabling, horsebox and caravan area visiting with friends, probably drank about ten cups of coffee and both of us were too wired to even think of sleeping. I remember us sitting in Ken and Stephen Pritchard's caravan until at least two in the morning. We drank coffee and playing 45 rpm records on a battery operated record player, those were the days.

We eventually went to bed about two thirty, I had to be up four hours later to muck out and feed the horses, tomorrow would be another day and the start of competition.

Chapter Fifteen

Six thirty the alarm goes off and I shoot out of bed to get my precious horses ready for their day's competition. Oro always had that deep little whinny when he saw me coming and Nappy would shake his head up and down wondering why he still had not received his breakfast. I fed them both, filled their water buckets and while they ate proceeded to muck out their stalls. I never had a problem with any of my horses while they ate, however, Oro always pushed his feed bucket all the way around the stall trying to get the final bits out of the bottom of the bucket, never once did he consider that I was in the way.

If he could lick a hole in the bottom of that bucket he would have done. I always had to take it away from him, which was often difficult because his nose was firmly pressed down in the bucket and he had a very large and heavy head. Oro was the kindest of horses and did not have a bad bone in his body. He was definitely one of the most-gentle horses I have ever been around.

After they had finished eating and I had completed mucking out the stable of each horse, we had brought a wheel barrow with us from home which was a God send as this is how I got all the manure out of each stable and wheeled it to the muck heap at the end of the stable block. I would always throw the clean straw, which we used in those days around the walls leaving the bare floor to dry out and freshen up.

CB

Nobody had heard yet about shavings, they would come to the horse world quite some years later, everybody used straw for bedding and at the end of each day while the horses were being fed their last meal of the day, the straw would be spread out with fresh clean straw added.

The wheelbarrow was also handy for bringing everything back and forth from the horsebox including the tack and grooming utensils.

It was now time to groom them both, put hoof oil on, tack them up and take them both down to the collecting ring and meet up with

Charles. He always turned out immaculately in his polished boots, white britches, lovely navy wasted riding jacket and velvet hard hat as we called them in those days. As usual, there was Mrs. Nuttall at his side with FiFi her treasured little miniature poodle tucked under her arm. The things that happened to that poor dog throughout the years, more on those fiascos later. Charles got on Napier first as he was the first to go in the novice ring and I jumped on Oro and walked, trotted and cantered him around too warm him up while Charles schooled Napier and jumped him in the collecting ring. Soon, Curly Beard was calling Charles's name and I rode Oro over to the edge of the ring to watch.

അ

Well there she goes again, as Charles entered the ring Mrs. Nuttall took off with the cigarette dangling out of her mouth and clutching FiFi under her arm around the outside of the arena. As Charles jumped over each one of the show jumps, there was mother throwing her leg high in the air and shouting "Hup". She did this at every fence, how she moved so fast I will never know and how Charles was never eliminated for outside assistance. However, they seemed to allow it because it was Mrs. Nuttal and the announcers would often say, "And that was a wonderful clear round from Charles Nuttall riding Napier, with of course the energetic help of his mother and FiFi". Everybody would laugh and Mrs. Nuttall would prepare herself for her next adventure around the ring with Charles in the next class. It always amazed me because she seemed to finish at exactly the same time that Charles did.

All of the riders and grooms expected this of her; they were always amused by this amazing character of our sport.

As I only had the two horses, I would often have a little time in the afternoons to go and watch the big classes which was always extremely exciting for me because our top riders would be there to compete. Harvey Smith, David Broome, Ted Edgar, Ted Williams, Carol Beard, Jean Goodwin, Malcolm Pyrah, Graham Fletcher, Caroline Bradley, Valma Milner, David Boston Barker, his brother William, John Bailey, Andrew Fielder, Anneli Drummond-Hay and more.

അ

People from many miles around would come out to watch these stars of our sport and then line up for their autographs and I would watch this often saying to myself with a smile, "many of these riders actually know my name".

This made me feel very proud that I was actually known by such unbelievable stars of the show jumping world, celebrities that millions knew of at home by the exposure they received on National television. Once the classes were over, I would head back to the stables to feed my two lovely horses and bed them down for the night. Then I would make my way to the caravan to sit with Charles while Mother as we called her, Mrs. Nuttall would cook us dinner with her cigarette ash constantly falling into the food. I can remember it sitting quite plainly on the top of an omelet and Charles told me to pretend is was black pepper, no wonder I ended up with asthma! Of course, as she was cooking, the two parrots in their individual cages squawked like crazy, the Siamese cat constantly growled, FiFi would not stop pawing the back of Mrs. Nuttalls legs wanting to be picked up and the Fox whimpered around our feet baring its teeth while its leash was tethered to the table leg.

I am amazed that I never ended up in a straitjacket. Later on, Charles and I would set off on our late evening jaunt around the horseboxes and caravans to see who was hosting the coffee and record playing party that night.

⋘

We rarely left the show grounds because very few had cars with them in those days as we had all arrived by and been driven to the shows in the horseboxes. It was rare indeed that we actually ever left a showground because everything we needed for the duration of the show was brought with us.

After four days at Balsall Common we were ready to set off home and said our goodbyes to lots of friends knowing we would see them all very soon at another show. I had a lot of work to do in getting everything ready, Charles helped a little also and together we loaded all that was left, Hay, Straw, Feed, tack, the wheel barrow etc...

Then I walked down to the stables and bandaged the horse's legs for travel, put on their travel rugs, tail guards and head collars. The ramp was already down to their part of the horsebox so I led them both from the stables, Charles took Oro and led him in and I immediately followed with Napier. Once we had the ramp up and everything was closed, we made sure that everything was secure in the caravan and attached it to the tow bar behind the horsebox. Mrs. Nuttall was already sitting in the driver's seat with a cigarette hanging out of her mouth revving up the engine. The small travelling zoo was back in the cab, we even had special hooks hanging from the ceiling of the horsebox to hang the parrot's cages.

CB

I was a little nervous and immediately thought, look out, here we go again terrorizing the roads of Great Britain as we head north on the M6 Motorway.

The first stop was just a mile down the road to fill up with petrol and I remember Mrs. Nuttall filling up two large tanks that came to about three pounds, petrol was extremely cheap in those days. Of course, while in the petrol station she had to go to the bathroom and I remember the door being broken, she asked me if I would stand outside while she went in, I will not go into detail but I remember that visit very well! Once she came out, into the smoke filled cab we climbed and set off toward the M6 and within a few miles we saw the signs, Motorway ahead. From Balsall Common we had only driven on country roads so the speed really did not exceed thirty-five miles an hour, however, with the motorway ahead I knew the worse was to come. Oh, I forgot to mention, in those days we did not have seat belts, I do not believe they had been invented yet so we knew no better.

We hit the motorway and with several grinding noises from the gear box, Mrs. Nuttall eventually got the Horsebox into high gear and we reached about seventy miles an hour. How that caravan stayed on the back I will never know, but it did. I think Charles double chained it onto the tow bar with padlocks so that it was secure enough for anything Mother threw at us.

CB

For sure she did not let us down and several times became blue in the face when she coughed to the point that there was no breath left in her lungs. I could not believe how those poor parrots in their cages stayed put on the hooks from the ceiling. They swayed from side to side and often smacked into each other and the squawking was deafening, we hardly noticed because we were too afraid of the horsebox going completely out of control, amazingly, it never did. If this had been in today's traffic, we probably all would have died.

Two and a half hours later we made it back to Withnell in once piece and even more amazing was that we had completed a round trip without being pulled over once by a police car. I have to say even to this day I am surprised those journeys did not give me an ulcer. We arrived home around lunchtime and I settled Oro and Napier into their stables. I then unpacked everything and put it into the tack room and feed room. Apart from having to feed the horses and bed them down later, I took the rest of the day off for a well-earned rest.

Chapter Sixteen

That year we had a fun show season and in August we headed for the Southport Show, a wonderful week that was held right on the coast with miles of golden beach across the road from the stables. This was one week in the year when a tremendous amount of riders brought their families and made it a lovely seaside holiday.

A lot of riders who did not have caravans hired them for the week and it was fun, excitement, competition and long rides on the beach. Southport Show was also known as one of the most prestigious Flower Shows in the country and gardeners spent days building their incredible displays to be judged and viewed by thousands of the public. It was also one of the most exciting show jumping events of the North West and riders came from all over the country with their horses competing at every level. Even the junior jumpers had many exciting classes over the three days to compete in and the best of juniors came out also including the Junior European Champion. On Thursday and Friday nights we had the floodlit jumping under lights, always a spectacular and exciting event. The evenings always started off with a large junior class followed by a Grand Prix.

I remember Lynne Raper competing on her two International mounts, Kiwis and Pierrot of which she had won the junior European Championship on earlier that year.

❧

Many other junior riders competed and from what I remember, Lynne won the J.A. Championship that first night, Thursday. On Friday many of us rode out on the golden sands of Southport Beach and it was a tremendous site for the beach goers to see some of the most famous horses and riders in the country cantering along the sand at the water's edge. Charles was riding Oro and I was riding Napier who was having a ball and was as frisky as could be with the wind under his tail we had a super gallop, he leapt in the air a couple of times, squealed and bucked, I loved it.

We passed a lot of our friends out riding that morning including Andrew Fielder and Vibart, Harvey Smith with O'Malley, Anneli Drummond-Hay riding Merely A Monarch, John Bailie aboard Dominick, David Broome with Mister Softee, the Barker brothers from North Riding in Yorkshire, Carole Bead with Mayfly and several others. I remember what a beautiful sunny morning it was and the public watching this spectacle were in awe owing to the amount of household names that were riding that day on their beach. It was very special for them and a wonderful experience for the horses and us. There is nothing like seawater to help with strength and healing on a horse's legs. The competition was incredible that week and we all had a wonderful time including Mrs. Nuttall and her miniature zoo that was firmly ensconced in her caravan.

ങ

She took care of us with the meals and light laundry and soon it was all over when Saturday evening hailed the close of a wonderful week in Southport.

Charles had won a couple of placings in the classes he had competed in and we packed everything up and headed home. It was always sad leaving Southport, not to mention that Formby where I was born and raised was only eight miles down the road. After Southport, we had a few local shows in September and then once again the British Show Jumping season had come to an end for us.

As an aside; this is my version of what Tracey, Andrew Fielder's sister sent to me regarding their trip to Madrid and Lisbon with the Team, May 1965.

Andrew had been selected with Vibart to join the British Show Jumping Team representing Great Britain in Madrid and Lisbon. It was May 1965 and what a team we had, our Chef-d'equipe was no other than the great Harry Llewellyn of Foxhunter fame. He brought a tremendous amount of experience with him of International Show Jumping.

Our team consisted of the great Peter Robeson with Firecrest and his wonderful groom and friend, Jo Hooley, Jo proved to be amazing and we learned so much from her, lessons that have lasted me a lifetime. Harvey Smith brought two of his horses Harvester and Rolling Hills and he also brought his groom Hazel who is still one of my closest friends ever.

CB

Johnnie Kidd brought his horse Bali Hai, Fred Welch brought Brule Tout and Judy Crago brought Spring Fever, a horse she had won the Queen Elizabeth II cup on.

We all met down at Folkestone as the horses were to be shipped across the English Channel by boat. My mother Helen had prepared and packed an enormous skip filled with food for us and also for the horses plus all of the tack. We also had our suitcases full of clothes and Andrew's riding attire for the two International shows.

This was the first time I had worked with Hazel, Harvey's groom and I soon found out that we had to take her under our wing owing to the fact that all she had with her was a packet of biscuits to last her the four nights and five days of this boat and train journey. Harvey had packed his horse's equipment but somehow forgot about Hazel guessing that she would be taking care of herself on the journey. Fortunately, Andrew and I had tons of food, which we shared with Hazel and we all decided to have great fun together and make the best of this journey ahead.

The riders were flying to Madrid, however, Andrew decided to travel with me and the horses, so glad he did as he was an enormous help and having him at our side helped us with him having celebrity status in our sport. I did not know what kind of luxury vessel I was expecting to take us across the Channel but it certainly was not the tiny thing I was looking down at from our vantage point.

CB

Firstly, the horses were put in crates and a crane picked them up and swung them through the air onto the deck of "Our Luxury Vessel." Thankfully the water was calm and we joined the horses on what now appeared to be our home on the water and set off for Boulogne. On arrival we went through the same procedure and once the horses were off the tugboat from Folkestone our train was waiting for us to take us to the Spanish border. We had nine horses in three boxcars and we soon discovered that we had to travel in the boxcars with the horses including sleep. Obviously this was not the first time we had slept with our four legged friends, however, not across France. Luckily for us, Jo Hooley, Peter Robeson's groom had done trips like this before and taught us how to pack everything in. There were three girls, myself, Hazel and Jo and we had Firecrest, Harvester and Rolling Hills with us in our boxcar. Firecrest was at one end and Harvester with Rolling Hills was at the other, we ate and slept in the middle.

The boys had the other two boxcars and we soon discovered the main problem for us all, there was no toilet. We also knew that the train had no scheduled stops, only to shunt, which was very noisy with banging and shouts etc. We did stop at times but we had no idea for how long and knew that if we jumped off the train, it may leave without us.

෴

Well, back to how we worked out the toilet facilities, we had buckets with us for the horses and decided that one of these would have to become our make shift Loo! We took to using the bucket when needed and slinging it out hoping that it did not go into the following boxcar. The other thing we were afraid of was getting locked in so we put rugs up over the doorways hoping that the rail workers would know we were in there. As the train traveled south, the climate changed to warmer weather and we all sat with our legs dangling out of the doorway, we were getting quite brave to this new way of travelling.

We did have a primus stove and camp beds and in some ways it was a lot of fun though I certainly could not do it today. The horses had settled nicely and did not seem to mind being cooped up, they really are amazing and adaptable animals. We had several milk churns full of water for them and bales of hay and straw. We mucked out as needed, throwing the dirty straw and droppings out of the door as we sped along hoping not to hit some poor local person either sitting at the side of the tracks or riding their bicycle to market.

We eventually arrived at the French/Spanish border where we had to change trains. Jo had warned us that we would have to take the horses and all of our belongings off this train, have all of our papers checked and walk the horses, equipment and everything we had across the border to the Spanish train.

෴

Well this train needed quite a few repairs before we could load the horses due to the fact that there were quite a few holes in the floor. Hammers, nails and other tools were required to patch everything and we just sat and watched telling jokes. At one stage, Andrew said we might have to pack everything on the horse's backs and ride the others all the way to Madrid. Poor Hazel thought he was being serious and was a little panicked until we assured her that he was pulling her leg. It was quite an experience travelling across the Spanish countryside seeing little old ladies in black sitting in the doorways of their little cottages in this sparse landscape with lots of heat. They had no air conditioning in those days and it must have been over a hundred degrees during the day in those little houses. It was hot on board the train and thank God the repaired holes in the carriage floor held up otherwise we would have arrived with no horses for the team to ride.

After five days and four nights at last we arrived in Madrid to see the luxury of horseboxes waiting for us to take us to the Club de Campo, what a luxury, we could not wait for real toilets and bathrooms with a nice bath to soak in. We had a whole yard allocated to each team with living quarters attached. Andrew stayed at the hotel with the rest of the riders and I chose to stay with the horses. We had lots of free days in between the Show Jumping Competitions with many parties organized including at the Embassies.

At one of these parties I met Ty Hardin the move star of many Westerns. Our riders won the Nations Cup and many of the other classes taking lots of glory home to England. It was quite an eventful trip and Hazel ended up losing her passport resulting in my mother Helen and her spending nearly a whole day at the British Embassy. The time came for us to leave Madrid and move on to Lisbon.

I did not find Lisbon as nice as Madrid and can remember eating in a stable, the flies were dreadful and in plentiful. We had competition every other day and the day in between we were taken on various trips. These included visits to a winery, and Olive farm and were treated to a bull fighting training farm we all had to go. Unfortunately, Peter Robeson was tossed and ended up in the hospital with concussion. This resulted in him missing riding in the Nations Cup. We also met Paul McCartney who was enjoying watching his fellow Brits compete in top class Show Jumping competition.

After five weeks of travel and International Horse Shows, we returned home, unfortunately the same way as we sent. We never had to travel that way again and nowadays with the modern air-conditioned and luxury laid out horseboxes, everyone has an incredible luxury that we never had. As Frank says we were part of "The Golden Age" and it is never to be repeated.

However, we did travel via horsebox and before Andrew was old enough to drive. Father would supply us with a drive from his Transport Company.

ᏨᏍ

I remember one drive bringing his wife along to Geneva and I had to sit in the middle. She had the worst body odor of anyone I have ever met and on our arrival at Dover, I abandoned our horsebox and decided to jump in and travel with Alison Westwood, the owner and rider of the great Maverick.

I hope you have enjoyed this little story of a time in my life with my brother Andrew Fielder and his great horse Vibart; it truly was "The Golden Age" of Show Jumping. Thank you for writing this book Frank and bring it all back to us once again, memories that will never be forgotten.

ᏨᏍ

I actually left the Nuttals and moved in with Peter and Valma Milner in Cuddington, Cheshire. Valma was the former Valma Craig who rode Bali Hai and Dark Victory to several successes and eventually sold Bali Hai to Johnny Kidd down in Surrey. I did not know at that time that one day I would be down in Surrey working for the Kidd's, however, I was with the Milner's some time and had lots of fun riding different types of horses as Peter was a dealer. I rode everything from ponies to hunters, to show jumpers and even some young thoroughbred's that had come straight off the race track. It was a fun time with Peter and Valma and because of the amount of horses that were consistently for sale, many characters visited the yard and I got to ride a lot of the horses for clients to see, which in most cases included jumping them, which I loved.

ᏨᏍ

By this time, my riding skills had really improved and I often caught Valma looking out of the window smiling when I was schooling or jumping one of the horses.

She was a super lady, lots of fun and a very good rider; however, she suffered badly with asthma, though at that time, I did not know how serious this was on her health. She and Peter had two daughters, Gillian and Janet, Janet was the baby. Gillian was a little character and absolutely horse mad, the double of her mother. She was probably about four at the time and spent most of her days wearing a riding hat, carrying a crop and jumping over everything in sight. If ever any of our feed and water buckets had gone missing, you could be sure Gillian had them with brooms, pitch forks, mops and anything she could get her hands on across them as her little jumps. She would gallop around smacking herself on the leg with the crop and shouting "hup" at every one of them. Sometimes she would hit one and fall, she never cried, just looked at the broom on the floor and called it a buddy rotten pig.

She also had a little Shetland pony by the name of Sheila, which she occasionally rode, however, I still think at that time she preferred to jump over her feed buckets and poles. That year, not long after I joined them, Peter and Valma headed down to Wembley and the Horse of the Year show with a couple of horses and I was left behind to look after the yard.

ᘓ

I felt sad and disappointed that I could not go with them, however, I knew my responsibility was at home taking care of everything while they were gone. I remember well the day they drove out of the yard in the horsebox and I waved them off down the road. I had vivid pictures in my mind of them arriving at Wembley and parking with the rows and rows of other horseboxes, stabling the horses and settling in with the crème de la crème of our sport. I knew that this particular week I would only see it on the B.B.C. and listen to that wonderful voice of Dorian Williams doing the commentary.

The following Sunday, Peter and Valma arrived home having sold one of the horses down at Wembley. The young horse they sold was All Trumps and was bought by Jean Davenport who eventually won the Queen Elizabeth II Cup on him, twice. She also represented Great Britain on several teams before eventually selling the horse to Michael Caine the movie star for his daughter Nicki to ride. The other horse that Valma had ridden in quite a few of the classes came back with them and for the life of me I cannot remember that horse's name. Several times, it almost comes to me and it is on the tip of my tongue. I can still see her though, a big bay mare that had a super jump in her and did have a few successes for Valma.

ᘓ

Soon it was my birthday month, November and I was to become 17 and started taking driving lessons.

Peter's sister, Christine let me drive her little green Mini now and again when she visited and I could not wait to get my license, I really thought that now I was driving I had at last become a man. My Birthday is November 5th, Guy Fawkes Day in the United Kingdom and Valma baked me a lovely Birthday Cake. I had never had a home baked Birthday Cake before and have never forgotten it. They had a live in Nanny called Christine who with Valma, Peter, the children and myself all sat around the table for a little birthday celebration, it was very special and a time I will never forget.

The Hunting Season got under way and Valma was a member of the Cheshire Hunt and each season one of the members had to become an opener and shutter of the farmer's gates as we galloped across their land. On the day it was Valma's turn she took me as a guest on a 14.2 hh pony we had, what fun that turned out to be.

This pony was a super jumper and jumped everything I put him at, ditches, hedges, gates and he even tried to overtake the Huntsman a couple of times. I had to hold him back like crazy because that was an absolute No No. On one occasion the hunt had gone through and I was about to close this gate while sitting on the pony, as the ground around the gate was very wet and muddy.

CƆ

I was just about to fasten it closed when I heard, thump a thump, thump a thump, thump a thump and over the hill came this enormous grey Cob with a lady in black silks riding side saddle shouting "Hold on, Hold on" which I did, having to open the gate once again. Well she cantered by me through all the mud and covered me from head to foot, I looked like swamp thing. Of course, I received no apology and she then slid off the horse and shouted "Young man, would you hold my horse while I go behind this tree for a pee" I froze with embarrassment and sort of stuttered, climbed off my pony and took the reins of her horse.

Off she went behind the tree as if it was an everyday occurrence with her, took care of her business and then asked me for a leg up. After about the fourth attempt I managed to get her back in the saddle of this enormous cob. I found out later when I told Valma the story, who by the way could not stop laughing, that it was Lady Astor, the great foe of Sir

Winston Churchill. Valma was also very amused when she saw me totally covered in mud and was even more amused when I told her how it happened. Very few people had cameras in those days. I only wish they had, can you imagine the pictures that I would have had from that day alone, but I will never forget my mud bath from Lady Astor?

CB

I remember one day Anneli Drummond-Hay visited us to try out some horses which was great excitement for me. I always had a crush on Anneli, ever since I had danced with her at the Southport Show Dinner Dance when I was twelve years old.

I still think even to this day I still have a crush on her. She was to me and always has been; the epitome of a lady and class. I can see her now pulling into the yard in a little red mini station wagon and when she had parked and got out my heart missed a beat. She spent most of the day with us and I rode a couple of horses for her to see and she eventually rode them herself to get a feel for them. From what I remember, she bought three from Peter that day and the following week he drove them down to her farm in Banbury and I, sadly, was left at home once again, oh well. I had lots of adventures with Valma and Peter, but the best one of all is yet to come and it happened on the moors bordering Lancashire and Yorkshire.

Chapter Seventeen

I remember a day when Peter was on the phone with Harvey Smith, they were great friends and business partners. Apparently, Harvey had a couple of horses Peter wanted and vice versa. I was excited because Peter asked me to go with him on this trip. We were to meet Harvey half way in a Pub car park. We set off from Cuddington in Cheshire late afternoon and drove east toward Yorkshire. About two hours later we arrived at our meeting point and Harvey was already there in his horsebox with his then wife Irene accompanying him. I had known Irene since I was eleven years old so while Harvey and Peter went about their business, we went inside the pub and bought a couple of Shandy's. For those of you who do not know what a Shandy is, it is English Lemonade, similar to Seven Up and a mixture of beer, quite delicious and refreshing actually.

Irene and I carried our Shandy's outside and sat on the wall having a nice conversation and sipping on our drinks while Peter and Harvey conducted their business. Well, it was not long before the patrons of this establishment found out that the famous Harvey Smith was outside with a horsebox full of horses. One by one they came out carrying their pints and before long there were about two-dozen beer drinking men all wanting a glimpse of and a handshake from the man himself, the famous Yorkshireman, Harvey Smith. Irene and I just sat on the wall laughing at this spectacle, as nobody knew who we were and obviously had no clue that we were part of the team. Harvey of course behaved quite well, but was not amused. He wanted to complete his business with Peter and head home, but he ended up signing several autographs and naturally everyone wanted to chat to him.

I suppose this went on for about half an hour and in the end, Harvey, nicely explained to the crowd why he was really here and excused himself. By then, several other people had arrived from the local village and were all standing there with silly grins on their faces in awe and star struck with the presence of Harvey Smith. Some had even awoken their children and brought them to see Harvey, several still in their pajamas, it was quite comical really. Peter stood and watched all of this with his signature cigar in his mouth and several people asked him who he was and if he was also a famous show jumper. He smiled and said, "No, I am not, but those two sitting on the wall are" meaning of course, Irene and myself. I then told them that Irene was Harvey's wife and that I really was nobody, but a couple asked for my autograph anyway. As they walked away and saw my name, they scratched their heads and looked back with very puzzled looks on their faces.

Harvey said later, you should have signed your name as Broomie, David Broome, we laughed. It was such a special evening for me and one I will never forget, it only seems like yesterday and I can still see that beautiful Yorkshire stonewall around the car park of the pub and the looks on the patrons faces when they realized it was Harvey.

There were so many special days at that time in Show Jumping and opportunities that came and went, that is why I will always call it The Golden Age.

One day at a show, Harry Bird who was the stud groom and driver for Lynne Smith from Warrington asked me if I would like to work with them and that I would also have the opportunity of perhaps riding some of her horses in Young Riders, I jumped at the opportunity. This was now my chance to start competing and my dream of becoming a Show Jumping rider was about to happen. I sadly left the Milner's and joined the stable of Lynne Smith.

I rode several horses a day while there and then one day Harry told me that he felt I was ready for competition. He was the former groom to another great from the Golden Age, a rider from Crewe in Cheshire by the name of Marshall Charlesworth. He had represented Great Britain on several teams with two horses, Smokey Bob and Rogation Boy. He had been on teams with the great Lt. Col. Harry Llewellyn who rode Foxhunter and Wilf White who rode Nizefella. Both of those riders had ridden on the Olympic Team in Helsinki in 1952 and until 2012 held the record as the last British team to win team Olympic Gold in Show Jumping.

છ

Other team members that had joined Marshall at various times were the great Pat Smythe, Alan Oliver, Dawn Palethorpe, Fred Welch and others.

I was excited at the prospect of competition and was still only seventeen; both Harry and Lynne decided to enter me in a qualifier at Balsall Common for the Young Riders Championship of Great Britain with the final to be held at Hickstead later that year. The horse chosen for this was a super little Grade A of Lynne's called Colour Bar. He was only 15.3 hh but had an enormous jump and loved his job. He was called Colour Bar obviously because of his color, brown and white, which in England was known as a Skewbald. I practiced hard at home with him for a couple of weeks until we clicked, I loved this little horse and every time I jumped him at home I visualized in my mind the pair of us jumping on a Young Riders team representing my country. The day arrived for us to leave on our journey to the midlands and the indoor arena of Balsall Common.

I had bought new riding breeches and a new jacket, as I already owned a fairly decent pair of Top Boots as they were called then and everything was packed into the horsebox for our trip down the M6. Lynne was entered in several classes on her other horses including Colour Bar, my class was not until the third day and I could not wait. It was a four-day show and I was to compete on Saturday and suddenly the day was here and I emerged from the Horsebox feeling like a million dollars in my new outfit and there was Colour Bar waiting for me.

We set off for the collecting ring and I was on cloud nine mingling and warming up with all those other riders. It was pure magic as my dream was now coming to fruition. After some schooling Harry walked with me toward the main arena to walk the course and I was quite surprised how big it was. The stands were filling up and there I was walking a show jumping course with several of our top young riders, many whom I had only watched compete in the arena.

Now, here I was walking the course and dressed to the hilt ready to ride against them. After the course walk and some pointers from Harry, I was back in the collecting ring riding Colour Bar over my final warm up jumps before heading down to the entrance of the arena. Suddenly it was my turn to go and there was quite a crowd filling the stands. I trotted down the middle of the arena looking around at the course and the judges rang the bell. I could feel my heart pumping in my chest, as I wanted to do well, my first thought was, oh my God, what if I forget the course. I cantered a circle headed through the start and there was the first jump in front of me and from there I just seemed to follow it around. I remember passing the entrance and saw Harry standing there nervously with a cigarette in his mouth and Lynne jumping up and down at the side of him.

Before I knew it, I was over the last fence and there was applause from the crowd, and I heard the commentator saying, "And that was a clear round for Frank Waters riding Lynne Smith's Colour Bar".

I actually did not know that we had jumped clear until the announcement and of course, Harry and Lynne were very pleased and excited. At the end of the class, there were five clear rounds of which I was one of them and we knew that the top three would qualify at this event for the final at Hickstead. I was second to go and I believed that I was Harvey Smith going against the clock, I had watched him do this so many times and tried to turn on a sixpence as they used to say, however, once too often and we ended up with a rail in the jump off. I did finish in a very fast time and I was the fastest with four faults. Unfortunately, three of the other riders jumped clear and I remember Sarah Roger Smith riding Foxtrot came out the winner.

I was fourth and very disappointed that I had not on this occasion qualified for the Championship at Hickstead. Harry told me that I had done very well for the first time out and that I would have another chance in two weeks at a show in Derbyshire, I could not wait and was determined this time that I would qualify. My advantage was that once riders and their horses had qualified, they did not enter in another qualifier. I had a very good horse in Colour Bar and new that the odds were now in my favor the next time we competed.

The following two weeks dragged because all I wanted was to ride in the ring again and as I was only allowed at that time to compete in the Young Rider qualifiers, there were few opportunities for me to be in the ring, Lynne had all the major rides and rightfully so, they were her horses.

❧

The day arrived to set out to the show in Derbyshire, I cannot remember the location but I do remember the day, it was very overcast with light drizzle.

Unlike Balsall Common it was an outside show, cold and wet but I did not care. In those days, all outside shows were on grass and the first thing we did was put studs into Colour Bars shoes. This time, before we schooled, Harry and Lynne walked the course with me and all of us in the arena had raincoats on, but I did not care, I wanted to win. Obviously, being outside, it was a bigger arena with what appeared to be more and bigger jumps than Balsall Common, but I was probably wrong, they were exactly the same. After the course walk and some very good advice how to ride it by Harry, we headed for the collecting ring with Colour Bar and started our warm up. He really did have an enormous heart and was a super little horse, whatever Harry put up for us, verticals and spreads, (Oxers as they are called today) he just cantered up and jumped them.

Curly Beard was the gate steward that day and I remember him saying as I rode up, "Eh lad, thay's come up in the world aint tha" and smiled wishing me luck as I rode in? Once again I totally focused on the course this time cantering around a little waiting for the bell. Suddenly, there it was and I set off at a decent canter giving Colour Bar the space he needed at each approach, just as Harry had told me to do and I felt he was jumping the moon.

CB

Once again, we finished with a clear round while Harry smiled and Lynne jumped up and down, she was quite an excitable girl. Lynne always wanted to park next to the Barkers from Northallerton, she had a soft spot for David Boston Barker who rode on the 1964 Olympic team with his brother William. Well, she eventually got her man marrying David some years later. Back to Colour Bar and my day in the Young Riders Championship of Great Britain qualifier in Derbyshire.

It was time to go into the jump off after a little more schooling in the collecting ring; this time eight had gone clear of which I was one. I believe I was third to go, the other two both had a rail and were on four faults, Harry told me how to ride the course and what corners to cut on the wet grass, I listened to his advice. The bell rang and off I set around the shortened course for the jump off and I remember they had left the treble in. I loved the trebles, jumping three fences at once with one stride after the first part, two strides after the second then jump out over the third. So far after the treble we were clear, I pushed on a to make up a little time and had three fences to go which one was a wall. We cleared the final three and as I landed I pushed Colour Bar like crazy and galloped through the finish with a double clear round in a pretty fast time.

ଔ

I was beside myself as were Harry and Lynne, I felt like I had just won an Olympic Gold medal and I could not stop patting Colour Bar, he was just magnificent on that wet surface. Of course, we had to wait for the other five riders to go, but my time was now the time to beat and they knew they had to go clear in a faster time to win. There was one more clear slower than me and the other three were on four faults, I was still leading. The last horse and rider came up to the gate and it was Prudence Langton, off she set and jumped clear a fraction faster than I had, she won the qualifier. However, I was second and we were all so excited because I had qualified myself and Colour Bar for the Young Riders Championship of Great Britain at Hickstead in July. As I rode in to the ring for the presentation of rosettes and the lap of honor, I was in a fog. That night, I could not sleep knowing that I was going to Jump in a Championship that many had won in the past and gone on to become International riders for their country.

Of course, that was my dream and all I could think of was being in the line up one day receiving my awards with Harvey Smith, David Broome, Anneli Drummond-Hay, Andrew Fielder, Ted Edgar, Malcolm Pyrah and other greats all sharing the lap of honor together as we rode with our Rosettes flowing in the wind on our magnificent horses. I really was a dreamer, however, I firmly believed that this was my time and that one day, all of my dreams would come true.

ଔ

On our arrival home to Warrington, I heard that John Smart had left the yard of James Heaton who owned three jumping horses, Mateus, Top Girl and Freddie H, Freddie H had formerly been ridden by Harvey Smith. Now that Mr. Heaton did not have a rider, I called him up and arranged an interview knowing that this would be an opportunity for me to ride on my own with no other rider as competition.

We arranged a meeting, I rode the horses, Mr. Heaton liked the way I rode and offered me the job, I was very excited and handed in my notice with Lynne Smith and moved to Penwortham one week later. I thought that I would still be able to ride Color Bar in the Young Riders

Championship at Hickstead later that year, however, it was not meant to be as I was no longer employed by Lynne and Harry Bird.

Chapter Eighteen

James Heaton owned a large Caravan Park in Penwortham, just outside of Preston in Lancashire; it was situated in a triangle of what used to be railway embankments. As you drove under the bridge, his office was immediately on the left and the Park stretched out ahead. Just before you arrived at the bridge was a stable yard with feed and tack room and to the side of that was a large field with a full set of Show Jumps and of course, turn out for the horses.

Freddie H did not do much anymore, he was semiretired but Mateus, a six-year-old was a character and we formed an immediate bond; he was a bay with a hogged mane. Top Girl was a different kind of horse, a super jumper and was a lovely dappled grey with a beautiful white mane and tail. I felt wonderful here as I was now totally in charge of everything, the taking care of the horses, the riding, the schooling and of course the rider of these horses at the forthcoming shows. I settled in very quickly and was taken under the wing of a Mrs. Manchester, who took care of me; she lived in one of the caravans. She often gave me lunch or dinner; sometimes both and she introduced me to a young recently married couple from Scotland, Peter and Fiona who happened to be her neighbors.

಄

Peter took a keen interest in helping me by coming out to the jumping paddock and adjusting the jumps in whatever way I wanted the while I was schooling.

He loved being involved and it was a great help to me as I did not have to keep getting on and off the horses when I was jumping to make adjustments. Fiona was expecting their first baby but loved to come out and watch all of the activities with the horses. They were wonderful long sunny days and evenings at that time and I would often look forward to Peter coming home from work and while Fiona cooked dinner, he would come out to the jumping paddock and help me with schooling, such

wonderful times and happy memories with a delightful couple as my
dear friends.

I traveled to several shows in the Lancashire, Cheshire and
Yorkshire area with Mateus and Top Girl and was often in the ribbons,
more so with Mateus, who I called Matty. He was a brave horse, hated
to touch a fence and was incredibly intelligent; he also never missed a
beat.

Within three months of riding for James Heaton he decided one day
that he was getting out of the horse business and planned on taking
Matty and Top Girl the following week to Leicester Sales. I was stunned
and did not want to part company with either of them, however, they
were not my horses so what could I do? Freddie H was like a pet to Mr.
Heaton and he was to live out his retirement right there in Preston, so
we loaded the two horses into the horsebox and set off for Leicester.

CB

I had a very heavy heart and wondered if I would ever see them again
and also I did not know what I was going to do. Fate played a wonderful
hand for me as a man called Ron Arnold from just outside of Watford
near London bought them both. The one thing I remember was what he
paid for the horses, two hundred and fifty pounds for Top Girl and three
hundred pounds for Matty. It was not uncommon in those days to buy
horses for this price, even those that had a record and talent.

He was asking me questions about the horses and I told him how sad
I was to be losing my friends and he said, "You don't have to, would
you like to continue riding them for me?" I could not have been happier
and we both agreed that I would go home to Preston, pack up and head
south. Mr. Heaton drove the horsebox back to Preston, dropped me off
at the house where I was lodging and the very next morning I was on the
train to Watford. Mr. Heaton made sure I had some money in my pocket
and also money for the train ticket and I was very happy to be now
heading south to join my friends.

On my arrival at Watford Station, Ron was there to meet me and
drove me back to his farm and introduced me to his wife Pat. Just outside
of the house was a very nice caravan, which was to become my home. I
had my main meals in the house and of course, took my showers in there
also.

CB

Ron owned a large pig farm called Russell's piggeries on the Hempstead Road and this was how he made his money.

The business was very successful and part of the farm was a really nice stable block with tack room, feed room and a large hayloft. After I had met Pat and put my belongings into the caravan, I walked down to the stables to meet another young man, Allan who worked there also. Ron had about nine horses all told and as soon as Matty heard my voice he pushed his head over the stable door and would not stop calling to me. Both of us could not have been more pleased to see each other and had a terrific reunion. Top Girl looked over, gave a slight whinny and went back to eating her hay. Alan was a great kid, about a year younger than myself and we got on very well, he was also a fairly decent rider and we shared all of the jobs and riding of the horses together, I was very happy there. From what I can remember I arrived there on a Wednesday and this coming weekend was to be our first show. Ron had a very nice horsebox and we loaded four horses including Matty and Top Girl.

I could not wait to show Ron how wonderful Matty was in the show ring and knew we would come back with several rosettes. I remember the show well as it was close to Aldershot. It was all new to me and a lot of different riders I had not met before. One of them was a Mrs. George Boone, her name was Vivian. Her husband was a retired Army Major.

CB

She was an older lady and he was one of the local committee heads of the British Show Jumping Society. Mrs. Boone was a tough lady who rode many different horses and I always seemed to get into the jump off against her as I did this day. I jumped clear with both horses and Matty was brilliant against the clock, he could turn on a sixpence and gallop around at great speed. In those days, the judges were very proper. They wore pin striped suits, shirts, ties and bowler hats. We also at the smaller shows had no electronic timers and everything was done with a whistle and stop watch.

At all the shows we competed I came across Mrs. Boone and we seemed to get into the jump off together. Today was no exception; Matty and I rode the course like a bat out of hell. Mrs. Boon by then was probably close to sixty and never took the risks I did as an eighteen-year-old, but somehow she always came out the winner. We knew, Ron knew and every other person knew I was much faster but we could never take the Red Rosette when Mrs. Boone and I were in the jump off together. We realized that it was impossible to fight the "Old Boys" club and I was basically the little upstart competing against the old school of a bunch of very close friends. I competed in three classes that day with Matty, came second to Mrs. Boone in two of them and the final class she was not it, so of course, we won.

∽

Alan and I had a terrific year with Ron Arnold and our great horses, though Matty turned out to be the number one horse in our stable.

He was a novice and I rode him in Grade B & C classes but he had tremendous potential to become a good Grade A horse. One day I was out riding him along a pathway adjacent to the M1 motorway, ahead of us was a five bar gate, probably about five feet in height. I thought, the only way to the other side was to jump it as it was locked, so I turned Matty around, cantered him at the gate and he took off. However, he hated to touch anything and as it was probably one of the biggest jumps he had ever jumped, I had all the confidence in the world in him; he rattled it quite hard behind. As the gate was fixed, it did not come down, his ears shot straight back and as he landed he was not happy, gave out a loud squeal and bucked like you would not believe.

I stayed with him and thought it was great fun, however, he was not in the least pleased. We continued our ride and on the way back it dawned on me that we would have to jump the gate again in order to get home.

Matty never forgot anything and when it came into view a sent him into a canter and headed for the gate. He was chomping at the bit, pushed his ears forward and I held him back knowing that he would be at that gate quicker than I wanted him to be. About three strides out, I let him have his head and I still do not know until this day how I stayed on because he must have jumped seven feet to clear that gate.

His talent was unbelievable and he did not have a stop in him and as we landed he squealed and bucked again, but this time in glee, he was so happy with himself and I was also having the best time ever. Matty was one horse in a million and he never, never let me down and always jumped clear with me in competition. I never let Alan ride him and he fully understood as did Ron, they both accepted that Mattie and I were a team and that is how it stayed the whole time I was with them.

As autumn arrived a terrible thing happened in England, a disease called Swine Fever spread through the country and everything was quarantined and we could not go to shows. Ron took every precaution he could but the disease caught up with Russell Piggeries and they were stricken with the disease. Every one of his pigs had to be destroyed and I always remember him and Pat crying, they lost everything, it was such a sad and hard time for us all. I never thought of the horses and believed everything would go on as normal and he would start again, how wrong I was. Ron called Alan and I into the house and told us that the horses had to be sold, as he just could not afford to keep them anymore. We were devastated and I did not know what to do. Ron told me that I could live in the caravan for as long as I wanted but I had to find a job and for three months I drove a taxi during that winter. The horses were sold and I never saw Matty or Top Girl or any of the other horses for that matter again.

○3

This was not a good time for me and I hated driving that taxi so I put my plan into action reading the Horse and Hound classifieds every week until in the spring I saw an advertisement at the Maple Stud in Ewhurst, Surrey. It was owned by the Honorable Mrs. Edward Kidd and her two children were Johnny and Jane Kidd successful International show jumping riders. I applied and was accepted as Groom/Rider with the younger horses, Johnny had his own groom who took care of the International horses, Grey Owl, Bali Hai and Sam Lord, he was also called John.

The Maple stud bred Hannoverian's and had two Stallions, the best and kindest of those was Maple Duelist who I rode and jumped often, we never took him to shows. Fred was the overall manager of the stud and stables and was one of the gentlest and kindest of people I ever worked with.

I helped break and ride the young horses and rode several a day, we had a nice indoor school and when people came to buy horses I normally rode them so they could see them perform. We had a female groom called Penny who worked with us as did Fred's son Ian. Ian eventually started working and driving for Johnny when John left. However, when we were at home, Ian helped us out in the yard with the other horses.

○3

We had many celebrities visit at weekends including George Lazenby who was to become a future James Bond, the actor James Villiers kept his horse with us, Oliver Reid would often come over, he was a friend of Johnny's and there were many others from film and television. Mrs. Kidd was the daughter of Lord Beaverbrook and she with her brother Max Aitken were the owners of the Daily Express and Sunday Express Newspaper.

Chapter Nineteen

Next door to Mrs. Kidd was a beautiful estate called Coxland and was owned by Mrs. Anne Harries.

Mrs. Harries was the mother of Jane Harries who was a beautiful debutante that became famous overnight when she ran off with and married her hairdresser from London, Gavin Hodge. Mrs. Harries decided that she was going to start a celebrity ball in London Called The Horse of the Year Ball and it would be held at the London Hilton on Park Lane. I had helped out in the past with some of her horses and she called me and asked if I would help her with the invitations for the ball and I told her that I would love to.

ଔ

I drove around there each evening, she would cook dinner and we spent weeks with her secretary Dorothy hand writing these beautiful invitations she had professionally printed.

We then put them into the envelopes for mailing. Even the envelopes were written by hand and I believe I still have the lump on my finger from all of that writing.

Mrs. Harries put me in charge of the Young Peoples Committee for the Ball and made me a Vice-President, I was very honored and felt extremely proud that I would have my name in several places in the magnificent souvenir program. We also set up tables at Hickstead and the Horse of the Year Show selling raffle tickets at two shillings a piece, the money was to go to the Olympic Equestrian Fund which would help send our riders to the Olympics. It was a fun time and I will never forget the beauty in the summer of Coxland, a magnificent estate in the heart of the Surrey countryside. It was situated in a lovely village called Ewhurst about a forty-minute drive from Guildford.

I had a little bungalow right next to the stables at Mrs. Kidd's and one night, we had a terrible commotion down at the stables, Grey Owl,

Johnny's top International horse came down with a twisted gut and sadly the vet had to put him to sleep.

He was a special horse and had been second in the Aachan Grand Prix with Johnny; Grey Owl was just ten years old.

ᙏ

I remember that morning well, there was such a heaviness over the stables and James Villiers came down to ride, I can hear his words of shock at the news when Fred told him. It took a while for Johnny to get over this terrible loss, especially as in those days, top International Grand Prix horses were hard to come by, Mrs. Kidd was also distraught by this and all of us felt like we had lost a relative. We continued our daily chores and even the horses seemed to know that something dreadful had just happened in our yard. I rode very somberly that day and we tried our best to carry on as normal, but it wasn't, nor would it ever be the same again without seeing Grey Owl's kind face looking at us over his stable door.

Mrs. Kidd suffered badly with Asthma and was often down at the stables with a portable oxygen mask. She carried a small cylinder of oxygen on her shoulder. Little did I know that I would be in a similar position in the not too distant future? I also did not know then that this was to finish my career with horses as a competitive rider. I was starting to suffer terribly with allergies and Mrs. Kidd was very sympathetic as she suffered also. My sneezing got more constant as in those days we used straw for bedding and of course the hay had to be shaken with a pitchfork or by hand before we filled the hay nets. I was inhaling all of this dust and sneezed consistently which was very exhausting for me, I even tried wearing surgical masks but it did not help much.

ᙏ

I can still see how black those masks used to be when I took them off from all of the dust in the air. The real trouble for my riding career started one morning, I was in Maple Duelist's stall shaking up straw for his bedding and I started to sneeze, all of a sudden, I was in panic mode and had my first asthma attack.

Having never had one before I remember reaching out with my hand trying to grab air into my lungs and my chest felt like somebody was pushing a pitchfork right into it. Fred helped as he had seen Mrs. Kidd several times in the same situation and tried his hardest to get me to relax. I was very much afraid as this was a first for me and I did not know how to get relief. Fred called Mrs. Kidd and she came down to see me suggesting that I see her doctor who knew her history with this problem. She made an almost immediate appointment and he sent me to Beechams Laboratory for allergy tests. They injected my arm with every allergy serum you can imagine and I reacted to every single one of them. Of course, my biggest allergies turned out to be horse, straw, hay, feed, and almost every type of dust one could imagine. I was also allergic to cats, dogs, feathers and one of my biggest allergies of all was cigarette smoke.

Fortunately, I did not smoke and even to this day I cannot be around a smoker without having a bad reaction.

CB

From all of this, they made up a series of injections for me to have twice a week to see if my immune system would fight this, it did not and my asthma got worse. I was about to face one of the most devastating days of my life. I was told by the doctors that if I did not give up horses and get totally away from them and their surroundings, this allergy problem could kill me by the time I was thirty. I was twenty-one at the time, almost twenty-two and was in total shock. My dream of becoming an International rider for Great Britain had just been shattered into a thousand pieces. I lost two of my friends to this who had the same problem, the rider who had sold Bali Hai to Mrs. Kidd for Johnny to ride, Valma Milner and later it took the life of the great Caroline Bradley. I was in a total fog and shocked not knowing what to do and Mrs. Kidd was a great supporter for me, she was wonderful.

She had Fred keep me away from as much as the dust as possible and all I did for a while was ride the horses. It helped a little until one day I was so stressed by this that I was finding it difficult to breath at all. Even going to bed at night was a dread for me because I could not breath when I lay down and I was getting depressed not knowing what to do. The choice had to be made and my life with horses or so I thought was about to come to an end. I left the Kidd's and went to stay with a dear friend of mine in London, May Charles, we had been friends since I was sixteen and we had formed a bond that has never been broken.

CB

She took care of me and I worked for Yardley the cosmetic company as a representative though I still with May visited the odd shows. Royal Windsor, The Royal International, The Horse of the Year Show at Wembley and others, May always came with me and loved it.

I also still helped Anne Harries with future Horse of the Year Balls and served on several of her committees including the Royal Ascot/Derby Ball. May and I had a couple of friends in Hertfordshire, Pat and Colin Priestman, Pat ran the Knebworth Park Show Jumping Club. One weekend, they invited May and I to go and stay with them as Pat was running a two-day show and thought it would be wonderful for me to see many of my old friends again. We drove to their house on Friday evening and we all went out to dinner and talked about the forthcoming weekend. I offered to help Pat and she would not hear of it, she just wanted May and I to enjoy ourselves and have fun.

Saturday morning, we left the house at about seven thirty for the show ground and Pat as usual was a total organizer and running around to every corner of the showground making sure that all was in order for the next two days of competition.

May wanted to help a little in the Secretary's tent, so she was quite happy helping competitors with their entries. Little did Pat and I know at that time she had forgotten one important person to help run the show, however, we were about to find out and my new career in the horse world was about to begin.

❧

At intervals during the hour leading up to the show starting, I kept saying to Pat, there must be something I can do and she kept saying no, just enjoy yourself. Suddenly, she grabbed my hand and said, "Wait a minute, come with me, I know exactly what you can do" and off we set off toward the judge's box. I was puzzled not being a judge, however, it was a caravan with two judges sitting in there whom I knew well. One was Bob Owen who looked at me and said, "Good morning Frank, what are you doing here" to which Pat said, he is our commentator? I froze having never held a microphone in my life, but one did not argue with Pat when she had her mind made up.

She put the microphone in my hand and I remember her words, "You wanted something to do now you have something to do so get on with it" of course I never expected this. Bob laughed as I said to Pat, "I didn't mean this, I do not like talking into a microphone" but she was adamant and humored me with, "You do not have a bad voice, so you are now our commentator" and she ran off to organize something else leaving me with the microphone. Bob Owen could not stop laughing and told me that I had asked for it and now I had no choice but to settle in and to do the best that I could. Three horses and riders had gone and I still had not said a word, Bob told me that if I did not start Pat would be over and would probably box my ears.

ೞ

Well, I turned the microphone on and started to talk and hated the sound of my own voice immediately and swore I would never offer to help anyone again.

By the time an hour had passed, I had settled down and was enjoying what I was doing and now had it in my mind that I was going to be a professional commentator. I thought, so fate has taken away my riding career but I can still be involved on another level and swore that one day I would work with Dorian Williams. Little did I know that I would and it would be no less than the Horse of the Year Show at Wembley three years later, a place I had dreamed about working when I first visited as that little thirteen-year-old boy. Now I have travelled the world and more than forty-four years later I am still announcing as a career with many, many more stories to tell about the complete turnaround in my life thanks too Pat Priestman. This will be the next book about me travelling the world as an International commentator and boy, do I have some stories to tell.

Now we go to the true meaning of "The Golden Age of Show Jumping" the Riders and Horses of that wonderful Golden Era who enthralled us all and brought show jumping into the living rooms of millions. In turn, the horses and riders became total celebrities, household names and icons in an era that will never be forgotten, enjoy.

Chapter Twenty

The Riders and Horses of The
Golden Age of Show Jumping

Harvey Smith

Harvey Smith and Mattie Brown

How can anyone forget the greatest character of our sport ever, Harvey Smith? I have known Harvey since I was eleven years old and the stories I have to tell of Harvey are so many.

From helping Blossom his groom in 1962 at Southport Show with O'Malley, Harvester, Warpaint and Sea Hawk. I have two Half Crowns still, one given to me by his mother and one by Mrs. Morphet, Sammy Morphet's mother.

ଓଃ

She and Mrs. Smith were best friends and went everywhere together and Harvey was best friends with Sammy. I was thirteen when I was given those, the equivalent of five shillings in those days 25 pence now. It was a lot of money to a young boy back then but I would not spend them, they are part of my thousands of memories of the Golden Age of Show Jumping. I still talk with Hazel almost once a month, Harvey's ex groom, she lives just outside of Leeds in Yorkshire and we often reminisce about the old days.

I even know how the famous two-finger salute at Hickstead came about; it is a typical and wonderful Harvey Smith story. Harvey showed up at Hickstead without the Derby Trophy and Douglas Bunn was not happy. To cut a long story short, Harvey argued with Douglas and told him that there was no point bringing the trophy as he was only going to win it again. Duggie wanted to put the trophy on display during the Derby meeting and Harvey did arrange for it to be brought down to Hickstead. Derby day arrives and Harvey was the last to go on Mattie Brown, the horse he had won the Derby on the year before, low and behold, he wins it again. The two-fingered salute was born and Harvey in no uncertain terms let the judge's panel and the officials know that he was taking no nonsense. Of course, there were some upset people in the V.I.P. box that day but in the end, Harvey won out and the trophy was his once again.

∞

Now, that two-fingered salute is and always will be the most famous gesture ever in the history of show jumping and will never be forgotten and will always be associated with Harvey. I even have a copy of his 45 RPM record he made singing "True Love" which he gave to me many years ago. Harvey also tried his hand at wrestling and was in his younger days an incredibly strong man, even tearing telephone books in two with his bare hands.

This year, 2013, Harvey, after becoming one of the most successful and colorful celebrities in the world of Show Jumping ever, assisted his wife Sue in training the winner of the Grand National, a lifelong dream of Harvey.

Harvey Smith with his son Robert on Warpaint

Once in a lifetime a special photograph is taken that leaves an impact on all involved. This has been the most requested photograph ever on the Golden Age of Show Jumping page. So many have asked to see it again, here it is, an incredible, incredible recording on paper of a very special moment frozen in time. A young Harvey Smith riding one of his great horses of the sixties, Warpaint. Here, Harvey rides with three-year-old Robert bareback on the Yorkshire moors overlooking Bingley, Yorkshire, Harvey's hometown.

ଔ

No hats, a son feeling completely secure with dad and a time when loose velvet caps where only worn in competition. In those days at some shows, there was a small fee to pay if a hat fell off, like half a crown, two shillings and sixpence. How could they not fall off, there was nothing to keep them on? Some had elastic under the chin, however, many riders cut this off, I know I did, hated that thin piece of black elastic cutting into your neck under the chin. I was lucky to help Doreen, "Blossom" with Warpaint, O'Malley, The Sea Hawk and Harvester at some shows in those days when I was on school holiday's, primarily at the Liverpool and Southport Shows, oh my, those were the days, I was in seventh Heaven! Enjoy this spectacular one of a kind photograph from the "Golden Age of Show Jumping". Also, as many of you may know, Harvey and his wife Sue train racehorses now with Sue as the head trainer. Together last year, they won the Grand National at Aintree with their horse 66/1 long shot Auroras Encore, who was ridden by jockey Ryan Mania The Grand National (officially known as the John Smith's Grand National for sponsorship reasons) was the 166th annual running of the Grand National horse race at Aintree Racecourse near Liverpool, England. The showpiece steeplechase, which concluded a three-day meeting (one of only four held at Aintree throughout the year), took place on April 6, 2013.

‹›

The maximum permitted field of 40 runners competed for a share of the £975,000 prize fund, which made the National the most valuable jump race in Europe. A massive congratulations to Sue and Harvey!

Eddie Macken

Eddie Macken On Boomerang

Eddie Macken is most definitely one of the greatest riders in Show Jumping history and was an absolute heartthrob in the seventies when he was almost unbeatable riding Boomerang.

This combination won everything together including helping the Irish Team win the Aga Khan Cup for three consecutive years. They also won four consecutive Hickstead Derby's 1976 through 1979, a record which still stands today. Eddie won two individual Silver Medals at the World Show Jumping Championships, one in 1974 riding Pele and another in 1978 riding Boomerang. In 1977 he won a Silver Medal at the European Championship riding Pele. Boomerang was definitely his most successful partner and together they won so many Grand Prix competitions all over the world and their partnership together lasted more than ten years at the top of their field. Eddie was on the Olympic team for Ireland at the 1992 Barcelona Olympic Games and again at the 1996 Olympics in Atlanta, he was the team trainer for Ireland at the 2004 Olympics in Athens.

Eddie moved to Canada in 2001 and based himself in Langley, British Columbia participating on the North American Show Jumping circuit. In 2008 he was invited to become the Irish Show Jumping Team Manager at the Dublin Horse show, it was Eddie's first time on an Irish team in more than ten years. The team was placed 2nd behind Great Britain. It is without a doubt that Eddie is one of the greatest show jumping riders ever. His career continues today spanning more than four decades, hundreds of world class Championships and he has most definitely won the respect and is admired by riders of every level all over the world.

CB

Eddie Macken's Boomerang was a horse in a lifetime. When he retired in 1980, his money winnings were in the region of a quarter of a million pounds, which at that time no other horse had achieved. To this day no one has equaled his record four consecutive victories in the British Jumping Derby at Hickstead, and he was, in addition, one of the most consistent Grand Prix horses of all time.

David Broome

David Broome on Mr. Softie

What is there left to say about David Broome, CBE and now retired International Show Jumping World Champion? In the Golden Age of our sport David and the great Mister Softee were the combination to beat. Together they won the European Championship, King George V Cup, Hickstead Derby and many other International Grand Prix's around the world.

One of the greatest show jumping riders in the history of our sport, David was born on March 1st, 1940 in Monmouthshire South Wales and his father Fred had him in the saddle almost immediately. He has been everything from European Champion to being B.B.C. Sports Personality of the Year in 1960. David says that his favorite horse of all was Sportsman. He still operates his stables at Mount Ballan Manor in Crick near Chepstow in Monmouthshire. David is still very active in the sport serving on many committees' and the administration side of the sport including running the Wales and West Shows at Mount Ballan Manor.

I wonder how many remember his groom of many years, Monica Baker. Monica married the Australian rider John Fahey and they moved to Australia with him after their marriage. I did hear that they had divorced and she was back in England. Below is just some of his winnings starting with the Individual Bronze medal riding Sunsalve at the 1960 Rome Olympic Games, that same year they also won the

Individual Bronze Medal at the World Championships in Venice. David eventually won the World Championship Individual Gold Medal held in La Baule, France in 1970 riding Douglass Bunn's Beethoven. The below results show what an amazing career he had on many different horses from a teenager until he retired from competition.

❦

David Broome, one of the best riders the world of Show Jumping has ever seen and he certainly helped make the Golden Age of Show Jumping what it was during that magical era.

Olympic Games

1960 Rome: Individual Bronze medal on *Sunsalve*

1968 Mexico: Individual Bronze medal on *Mister Softee*

1988 Seoul: Equal 4th place on *Countryman*

World championships

1960 Venice: Individual Bronze medal on *Sunsalve*

1970 La Baule: Individual Gold medal on *Beethoven*

1978 Aachen: Team Gold medal on *Philco*

1982 Dublin: Team Bronze medal on *Mr Ross*

1990 Stockholm: Team Bronze medal on *Lannegan*

European championships

1961 Aachen: Individual Gold medal on *Sunsalve*

1967 Rotterdam: Individual Gold medal on *Mister Softee*

1969 Hickstead: Individual Gold medal on *Mister Softee*

1977 Vienna: Team Silver medal on *Philco*

1979 Rotterdam: Team Gold medal on *Queensway Big Q*

1983 Hickstead: Team Silver medal on *Mr Ross* 1991 La Baule: Team Silver medal on *Lannegan* FEI World Cup

World Cup Jumping League Winner 1979/80 with *Queensway Big Q* and *Sportsman*

World Cup qualifier wins

1978/1979 's-Hertogenbosch on *Philco* 1979/1980 Birmingham on *Sportsman* 1979/1980 Wien on *Philco*

1979/1980 Bordeaux on *Queensway Big Q* 1979/1980 Amsterdam on *Sportsman* 1980/1981 Olympia (London) on *Philco* 1981/1982 London (Olympia) on *Philco* 1981/1982 Dublin on *Mr Ross*

1983/1984 Amsterdam on *Last Resort*

1966 Hickstead Derby winner on *Mister Softee* King George V Gold Cup

1960 on *Sunsalve*

1966 on *Mister Softee*

1972 on *Sportsman*

1977 on *Philco*

1981 on *Mr Ross*

1991 on *Lannegan*

International Grand Prix wins include:

1960 Dublin on *Sunsalve*

1967 Dublin on *Mr Softee*

1968 Dublin on *Mr Softee*

1970 La Baule on *Beethoven*

1973 St. Gallen on *Manhattan*

1975 Olympia (London) on *Philco*

1977 Dublin on *Philco*

1979 Amsterdam on *Sportsman*

1979 Dublin on *Sportsman*

1981 Olympia (London) on *Philco*

1980 Olympia (London) on *Philco*

1983 Amsterdam on *Last Resort*

1981 Dublin on *Queensway Big Q*

1981 Spruce Meadows on *Queensway Philco*

1981 Horse of the Year Show (Wembley Arena) on *Mr.*

Ross

Greg Best

Greg Best - U.S.A. on Gem Twist

Greg was born on July 23, 1964 in Lynchburg, Virginia. He is an equestrian competitor and coach in our wonderful sport of show jumping and is best known for winning two silver medals for the United States in the 1988 Summer Olympic Games in Seoul, South Korea riding his incredible partner, Gem Twist. He competed at top International level in Show Jumping for two decades and from a virtual unknown to an Olympian it took him just eighteen months. He and Gem Twist clicked immediately and soon became one of the greatest combinations of Show Jumping Horse and Rider in the world. Together they won Individual and Team Silver Medals at the Seoul Olympics in 1988 and were in the final four at the World Equestrian Games in Stockholm, 1990.

೮೮

Greg was crowned Rookie of the Year and Gem Twist was Horse of the Year, just a few of the amazing accomplishments they achieved together. They won many Grand Prix's, medals for the United States at the Pan American Games and competed with great success on several Nations Cup Teams. He is also New Zealand's Chef d'equipe, team selector and high performance manager. In these capacities Greg has taken teams to two Olympic Games, two World Equestrian Games and many other International Events. He now lives permanently in New Zealand spending most of his year conducting instructional clinics of every level all over the world including his home country, the United States.

In 1992, Greg suffered a fall that shattered his shoulder. After this, he moved to New Zealand, where he rode for the New Zealand League, winning the World Cup Series and the New Zealand Show Jumping Grand Prix Series. He has also served as a New Zealand National Show Jumping Selector, a National Show Jumping Coach and a member of the New Zealand Show Jumping High Performance Committee. Greg coached New Zealand's jumpers for the 2004 Summer Olympic Games in Athens. Between 1987 and 2003, he also garnered 6 FEI World Cup wins. He now conducts coaching clinics in the United States, Canada and New Zealand. Apart from Gem Twist, he has ridden Santos and Entrepreneur which have been among his champion horses.

◌※

I saw Greg at Lamplight Equestrian in Chicago about six years ago; he had come over from New Zealand to coach some of the local Chicago riders and also to compete for the two weeks. He looked amazing and it somehow added a kind of magic to the two-week show having such an amazing legend with us. He is one of the nicest guys, still a beautiful rider, very charming, an amazing knowledge of both the practice and theory of Show Jumping and it was such a pleasure to spend two weeks with him and introducing him once again into the Show Jumping Arena of the United States. Here are some of Greg's major accomplishments.

1984 - Won the North American Young Rider Championships

1985 - USET Talent Derby

1986 - USET Foundation Lionel Guerrand-Hermès Memorial Award

1987 - American Grand Prix Association Champion, Grand Prix of Florida, Grand Prix of Tampa

1987 - Team Silver Pan American Games

1988 - Individual and team silver for show jumping in Seoul Summer Olympic Games

1990 - Final four in the World Equestrian Games

2001/2002 season - winner FEI World Cup Jumping - Pacific League - New Zealand

Frank Waters

Paul Darragh

Paul Darragh - Ireland and Heather Honey

Paul was born on April 28th, 1953 and would have celebrated his 61st birthday this year. I knew Paul back in the late sixties, early seventies when he rode with Harvey Smith. He, along with Willie Halliday where Harvey's two stable jockeys in Bingley, Yorkshire.

What a delightful man he was, always smiling, great sense of humor and even then was the epitome of a gentleman and future star of show jumping.

ଔ

Paul eventually became one of the mainstays of the Irish Show Jumping team including becoming a member of the winning team for the Aga Khan trophy three years in a row from 1977 to 1979. He rode the mare Heather Honey on those teams and they also had many other national and international successes together.

In an amazing international career that spanned a quarter of a century, he joined with Eddie Macken, Con Power and James Kernan on the Irish team that captured the public imagination, as they became absolute heroes of Ireland.

A full 20 years after the first of those successes, Paul was on the team that won the trophy again in 1997, his last major win on an Irish team. Other highlights included wins in the Hickstead Derby on Pele and the Dublin Grand Prix on Carrolls Trigger. In total he represented Ireland 54 times in Nations Cups.

Paul tragically died suddenly at his home in Meath aged 51 on January 3rd, 2005. Paul is a tremendous loss to Ireland, the world of Show Jumping, his family, friends and colleagues around the world.

At the time the Equestrian Federation of Ireland (EFI) president Avril Doyle said, "It was a great shock to learn of Paul's untimely death.

He will be remembered as one of this country's show jumping greats, for his talent, commitment and professionalism, and his achievements on both the national and international stages stand as his testimony.

CB

On behalf of the EFI and myself, I would like to extend heartfelt sympathy to his wife Jane, daughters Linda and Amy, his son Andrew, his father Austin, and his extended family." As long as I am around, the incredible stars of yesteryear like Paul Darragh will never, ever be forgotten.

H.R.H. Princess Anne The Princess Royal

H.R.H. Princess Anne, Princess Royal and Doublet

H.R.H. Princess Anne was almost born into the saddle, as was most of the Royal Family, while her brother Prince Charles followed and eventually took up Polo; Princess Anne was in love with the exciting world of Eventing.

ೞ

She competed successfully in Pony Club events and at the age of twenty-one she represented Great Britain, in the European Three Day Event Championship winning the Individual Title. She was also that year, 1971 voted the B.B.C. Sports Personality of the Year. Princess Anne became a regular member of the British Three Day Event Team and won Silver Medals in both the Individual and Team events at the European Championships riding Doublet, her mount when she won the European Individual Championship. Doublet was a homebred chestnut bred by her mother, Her Majesty the Queen. She has competed throughout the world at major Three Day Events including Badminton, Burghley and of course, the Olympic Games. Credit must go to her in many ways owing to the fact that she was hounded by the press who consistently waited for her to have a fall. The pressure she endured while competing was amazing and no other rider had to go through this. That is why those of us in the sport admire her so much because each time she went out to ride, her determination, talent and drive brought her many times through her own skills to the winner's circle.

Princess Anne made history in 1976 becoming the only Royal to represent her country at the Olympic Games. She was a member of the British Three Day Event Team in Montreal, Canada and rode the Queen's horse, Goodwill, a horse that was purchased from Trevor Banks, who had shown many top International Horses with various riders throughout the world.

From 1986 until 1994 Her Royal Highness became the President of the F.E.I. known as the Federation Equestrian Internationale.

She was married to Mark Phillips and one of their children followed in her mother's footsteps to also become a World Class Three Day Event rider, Zara Phillips. Princes Anne is now married to Vice-Admiral Sir Timothy Laurence.

I was sitting next to Dorian Williams at the Horse of the Years Show the night she was introduced in the Cavalcade as the Three Day Event European Champion. She was introduced before Ann Moore, the Ladies European Show Jumping Champion of the same year. They were the last two to come into the arena. All of the horses, riders, celebrities and foreign riders had entered the arena when the band played some exciting entry music. The spotlights were directed to the entrance of the arena and Dorian Williams shouted out in his wonderful voice, "Ladies and Gentlemen, Three Day Event European Champion, Princess Anne," it literally brought the house down. When the excitement had subsided a little above the noise, he announced, "Ladies European Show Jumping Champion, Ann Moore." Again, there was another eruption as the two Anne's took center stage in the middle of the arena before he read the "Tribute to the Horse." It was another magical night at Wembley that I will never forget.

Nick Skelton

The Great Nick Skelton

Nick Skelton was born on December 30th in Bedworth, England and was riding at the young age of eighteen months.

I remember when Nick first started to be noticed when he rode for Liz and Ted Edgar, he was an enormous talent even then as a young teenager. This was after taking his pony to them for help when he was just fourteen. Nick had many, many successes both on the National and International level riding under the Everest Double Glazing name, the major sponsors of Ted and Liz's horses. Some of his early successes were on the great Everest Maybe. From the beginning, Nick was popular with his peers and riders from around the world immediately spotted his talent. Nick rode for the Junior European Team in 1974 and 1975 winning two Silver and one Individual Gold Medals in the Junior European Championships. Since then, he has competed all over the world including winning three gold medals, three silver medals and three bronze medals at the European Show Jumping Championships. In 1980 he competed in the Alternative Olympics and helped Great Britain win a team Silver Medal.

While riding for Liz and Ted, he broke the British High Jump Record at Olympia jumping 7 foot 7 inches on Lastic. The following year he broke into the senior British Show Jumping Team riding St. James. Nick left the Edgar's and started up on his own in 1985 and the rest is history. He defied all odds after breaking his neck in September of 2000, which he and everyone else at the time believed this had ended his riding career.

∞

Nick being Nick recovered and started competing again two years later when he again partnered Arko III going on to win the British Open Show Jumping Championships in 2004.

From that time, Nick has just become better and better and fulfilled his dream at last year's Olympics in London when he led the British Team to a Gold Medal, the first since 1952. He was also awarded the Officer of the Order of the British Empire (OBE) in the 2012 Birthday Honors for services to equestrian sport by Her Majesty the Queen. Inclosing Nick, I can only say, "You have come a long way baby."

Just look at some of the amazing successes that Nick has had around the world, and this only touches on the winnings of this amazing Equestrian who started his career during the "Golden Age" of our sport.

Olympic Games

2012: London. Team Gold medal with *Big Star* Alternative Olympic Games

1980: Rotterdam. Team Silver medal with *Maybe* World championships

1982: Dublin. Team Bronze medal with *If Ever*

1986: Aachen. Team Silver medal and individual Bronze medal with *Apollo*

1990: Stockholm. Team Bronze medal with *Grand Slam*

1998: Rome. Team Bronze medal with *Hopes are High* European Championships

1985: Dinard. Team Gold medal and individual 4th with *St. James*

1987: St. Gallen. Team Gold medal and Individual Bronze medal with *Apollo*

1989: Rotterdam. Team Gold medal with *Apollo* 1991: La Baule. Team Silver medal with *Phoenix Park* 1993: Gijon. Team Silver medal with *Dollar Girl* 1995: St. Gallen. Team Silver medal with *Dollar Girl* 2011: Madrid. Team Bronze and individual Bronze medal with *Carlo 273*

Junior European Championships

1974: Lucerne. Team Silver medal with *Maybe* 1975: Dornbirn. Team Silver medal and individual Gold medal with *O.K*

Volvo World Cup Final

1995: Gothenburg. Winner with *Dollar Girl*

Hickstead Derby

1987: Winner with *J Nick*

1988: Winner with *Apollo*

1989: Winner with *Apollo*

King George V Gold Cup

1984: Winner with *St. James*

1993: Winner with *Limited Edition*

1996: Winner with *Cathleen III*

1999: Winner with *Hopes are High*

Nick Skelton London Olympics 2012

These are just some of the top horses that Nick has ridden through his amazing career:

Maybe, If Ever, Apollo, St. James, Major Wager, Top Gun, Grand Slam, Phoenix Park, Dollar Girl, Limited Edition, Showtime, Tinka's Boy, Hopes are High, Russel and Arko III.

Skelton's current top-flight horses are Big Star, Carlo 273 and Unique, all of which are owned by Beverley Widdowson.

Peter Robeson

Peter Robeson on Firecrest

Peter Robeson was born on October 21st, 1929 and followed in the footsteps of his father Gilbert who was a pre-war show jumping Champion. While still a teenager, Peter made his first ever International appearance and in 1952 narrowly missed being selected for the Olympic Show Jumping Team in Helsinki, Finland. However, he did make his Olympic debut four years later in Stockholm where he won a Bronze medal as a member of the British Show Jumping Team. He rode Pat Smythe's Scorchin, which she kindly lent to him, she rode her other horse on the team, Flanagan, their other team member was Wilf White with Nizefella.

※

Eight years later he won a bronze medal in a jump off with Australia's John Fahey. He partnered Firecrest, a horse he owned and from thereon formed an amazing partnership with this horse. Together they won the King George V Gold Cup at the Royal International Horse Show in 1967 and from together won everything imaginable. Peter rode in the Olympics again at the age of 46 in the 1976 Olympics riding Law Court where he was seventh in the team event and fourteenth in the individual. Peter represented Great Britain more than eighty times during his illustrious career of more than forty years at the top.

He is married to Rene who was a member of the Rothschild family and this helped him retain his amateur status throughout his career as his peers all turned professional. He is a former director of the British Show Jumping Association and is also listed with them as a Show Jumping Trainer. Peter is now retired from show jumping and trains racehorses with his wife Rene.

Elizabeth Broome-Edgar

Elizabeth Broome-Edgar known to us all as Liz Edgar - seen in action here on Forever Liz as she is affectionately known to us all was born in Cardiff, Wales on April 28th, 1943 and was Christened Elizabeth Broome, younger sister of World Champion David Broome. As a young rider she made a name for herself on several horses including Bess, she also won the Young Riders Championship of Great Britain in 1960 and 1961. She rode at her very first Horse of the Year Show at age twelve in 1955 when it was held at Harringay.

❦

Liz, like her sister Mary and brothers David and Fred Broome all started riding at very early ages in life under the guidance and training of their father Fred Broome Senior. He was an amazing man and travelled the circuit almost his whole life training and supporting his Show Jumping Family. Fred had an amazing eye for a horse and guided all of his children to become experts in their field riding the best of horses.

Elizabeth Broome married international show jumper Ted Edgar and for the rest of her career she was known to us all as Liz Edgar. She represented Great Britain on many occasions including riding on sixteen Nations Cup teams and lifted the trophy in 1979, 1980 and 1985. She is winner of the Queen Elizabeth II Cup a record five times, 1977, 1979, 1981, 1982 and 1986. Liz also made history by becoming the first woman Show Jumper to win the Aachen Grand Prix, known as one of the most difficult in the world riding her brilliant horse, Everest Forever. Soon after they formed, the Everest Stud in conjunction with Everest Double Glazing Company; suppliers of Conservatories, Windows and a leader in Double Glazing. In 1988, Liz had a horse called Debutante II and she had numerous National wins including Merrist Wood, Wales and West, Royal Lancashire, the Jersey Championships and many other National wins.

In 1975 Liz won the National Ladies Championship at the Royal Windsor Horse Show riding Everest Maybe and she won it again in 1982 riding Everest Forever.

 os

Liz decided to ride on the American Tour in 1977 and won the prestigious New York Gran Prix on Everest Wallaby. In the latter part of her career, probably the greatest horse she ever rode took Liz to titles all over the world, Everest Forever, the horse on which she won the Aachen Grand Prix. Together they became a household name and were sixth in the 1982 World Cup Final in Gotheburg as well as many National and International wins.

Her daughter Marie is following in her mother's footsteps and helps now run the Everest Stud in Warwickshire. It has now become one of the most sought after training establishments and has trained many of the world's leading International Show Jumpers including Nick Skelton Frank Sloothaak and Lesley McNaught. Since retiring from competition, Liz has remained heavily involved in the sport including serving on the Rules Committee of the British Show Jumping Association. Liz Edgar is one of the true pioneers of the Golden Age of

Show Jumping and I am delighted to have this incredible lady of Show Jumping history in my book.

Pat Smythe

Pat Smythe on Flanagan

Pat Smythe was born on November 22nd, 1928 and was christened Patricia Rosemary Smythe. Throughout her career she was known as just Pat Smythe and became a household name. Every little girl at that time fell in love with horses and they all wanted to be Pat. More than anybody at the time, Pat Smythe put show jumping on the map in Great Britain and eventually this spread throughout Europe. Pat's first time riding was on a pony called Bubbles which happened to be her brother's pony and she learned to ride very quickly showing talent even at that young age.

CB

Her parents, Eric Hamilton and Frances Monica Smythe bought her a Dartmoor x Arab pony called Pixie. Pat's mother was often sent Polo Ponies from a family friend, Johnny Traill for breaking and then to be schooled for Polo. As Pat got older, she helped in the schooling and breaking of these ponies, which gave her tremendous experience and patience with horses. Pat eventually moved to the Cotswolds and this is when she first gained her taste for Show Jumping and found a horse called Finality. They competed together at many gymkhanas and Finality suffered numerous injuries but this did not stop them from continually competing together and winning. Finality was owned by a family friend Johnny Trail and due to financial problems; the horse had to be sold. This was a blow to Pat but she sprung back with a mare called Carmena and although Carmena was a talented and successful horse for Pat, she always said that she never had the same closeness and relationship that she had with Finality. A tremendous string of horses was to follow which led Pat to become one of the most successful riders in the world achieving many firsts for a woman including being invited to become a member of the Olympic Team, the first Equestrian woman ever to do so.

In 1949, Pat bought Prince Hal, an ex-racehorse who was initially called Fourtowns. She renamed him Prince Hal after the role of Sir Laurence Olivier and he became the first of a tremendous amount of horses for Pat that went on to International success.

She then purchased Tosca, which together they won many medals and show jumping competitions of the day including several trips abroad with the British Team. When she retired Tosca in the 1950's she bred several foals from the horse including Lucia, Favourita, Flamenca, Laurella, Chocolate Soldier, Melba, Sir John and Three Card Trick. Later on in her career she rode such great horses as Flanagan, a horse she won the Olympic Team Bronze Medal on in the 1956 Olympic Games in Stockholm and many other National and International successes. At one time Flanagan was owned by Robert Hanson a haulage contractor from Huddersfield in Yorkshire.

He also at one time owned O'Malley ridden by Harvey Smith and Merely A Monarch ridden by Anneli Drummond-Hay. Pat also had such great horses as Brigadoon, Scorchin, Mr. Pollard, Ocean Foam and Telebrae. Scorchin was loaned by Pat to Peter Roberson to ride on the same Bronze winning Olympic Team as her in Stockholm in 1956. Pat Smythe was the first woman ever to win the Hickstead Jumping Derby riding Flanagan in 1962 and the second person ever to win it, Seamus Hayes was the first in 1961 with Goodbye. Pat Smythe became the author of many books and little girls all over the country bought these with a dream of one day becoming another Pat Smythe. In 1960 after the Rome Summer Olympic Games she married her childhood friend Sam Koechilin and from then on was known as Pat Koechlin-Smythe.

ଓଃ

Sam was Swiss and together they moved to and lived in Switzerland, it was here that she wrote many of her books, which included several books for children about ponies. When Sam passed away in 1986, Pat moved back to her beloved Cotswolds and died there on February 27th 1996 at age 67 of heart disease. She will never be forgotten as a woman who made tremendous strides in the sport of show jumping and paved the way for women to become equally competitive against men. A true Pioneer, who is now part of the history books and was a true legend and instigator of the Golden Age of Show Jumping.

Iris Kellett

Iris Kellett - Equestrian and Trainer Extraordinaire seen here on Morning Light

Iris Kellett was an only child and her father was a veterinarian in the British Army and retired to join the family business, a large Drapers shop, famous in Dublin - Kellett's of George Street.

❧

He purchased the old British Army Cavalry stable at Mespil Road in Dublin and turned it into a wonderful and well-known riding school. He was known for his knowledge and skill with horses and had a very gentle way of breaking and training youngsters. This was a skill that Iris perfected and became brilliant at years later. Iris certainly became the most influential and respected person in Irish Show Jumping with a reputation that was known and admired internationally. Both parents encouraged Iris in her endeavor of horses from a young age, however, she lost her mother when she was in her teens, then her father became ill and she totally dedicated herself into the world of the horse.

Her education was at St. Margaret's School in Mespil Road, which allowed her to come home every day and take lessons at the Stables. Iris decided not to go to college when she left school as she wanted to dedicate herself to her riding career and the operation of Mespil Riding School. Show Jumping being one of few sports where men and women compete equally encouraged Iris to become equal in the sport to any man or woman on horseback. She excelled her riding career to many victories both on the National and International level. Early in her career, the pony strided-horse Starlet took her to a level that many thought impossible. However, it was her beloved partnership with Rusty that took her to new heights including winning at the White City, London in 1948 at age 22, the year the Olympics where held at Wembley.

In 1972 Iris sold the riding school on Mespil Road knowing she needed more land to improve and bought acreage in Kill, County Kildare building what was then the finest Equestrian Centre in Europe. Throughout her illustrious career Iris Kellett won many prizes for show jumping and trained some of Ireland's best-known horses and equestrians, amongst them, Eddie Macken and Paul Darragh.

At the height of her career, she rode in a male-dominated world of show jumping. Iris won the Grand Prix at the Dublin Horse Show and the Princess Elizabeth Cup at White City in 1949 on Rusty, when she was just 22. She again took the Princess Elizabeth Cup in 1951, and in 1969, in Dublin; she won the Championship of Europe riding Morning Light in Dublin. This definitely put her in the league of one of the top riders in the world at that time in show jumping history.

The Princess Elizabeth Cup is now the famed Queen Elizabeth the II trophy competed for at the Royal International Horse Show. Iris was 85 when she died in March of this year, 2013 an amazing ambassador to the Golden Age of Show Jumping.

Nelson Pessoa

Nelson Pessoa - Brazil

Nelson Pessoa Filho was born on December 16th, 1935 and was one of the first Brazilians to compete at international level in the sport of Show Jumping owing to the fact that at this time in the sport, show jumping in Brazil was dominated by the military. As a junior, he took part in the International of Rio de Janeiro and three years later joined the Brazilian team to compete in his first international show at the International of Buenos Aires, Argentina. He had his first International victory in Mar del Plata. Neco, as he is known to his friends, set the strides for Brazilian Show Jumping when he competed in the 1956

Olympics. He was fifth at the 1964 Summer Olympics in the individual event in Tokyo.

Nelson moved to Europe in 1961 and in 1966 won the European Show Jumping Championships winning twice at Hickstead. He was second in the 1984 Show Jumping World Cup and in 1991 was second riding Special Envoy. He founded the famous Equestrian Academy at Haras du Ligny in Fleurus, Belgium and has many successful students including Alvaro de Miranda Neto and Athina Onassis Miranda. His son Rodrigo is an Olympic Gold Medalist in Show Jumping. Nelson is also the founder of many Pessoa Brands including saddles, bridles, girths, blankets and tack.

Nelson rode many horses in international competitions and apart from Gran Geste, Huipil gave him some of his best results including World Championships and the Olympics. Huipil was an Argentinian bred horse; they were fourth at the 1966 World Championships in Argentina and fifth at the Tokyo Olympics in 1964. Nelson won two Gold Medals and one silver at the Pan-American Games, was seven times winner of the Hamburg Jumping Derby, won the Hickstead Derby three times and a former European Champion. Gran Geste was the first horse Nelson had his best International successes on including three-time winner in Hamburg, European Championship and the Hickstead Derby to name a few, he died at age thirty-two. His other successful horses included Huipil, World Championship and Olympic mount.

∾

Espartaco was twice winner of the Hamburg Jumping Derby. Passop was a Russian bred horse that he also took to the Olympics in Mexico City and winner of International Championships in Germany. Nagir, won around twenty-five International Grand Prix's. Miss Moet, together they won seventy-two Puissance competitions including winning the Puissance in Bordeaux at age twenty. Special Envoy, with lots of victories for Nelson, this horse eventually became the first successful mount for Rodrigo. Chouman, together they gained a fifth place at the World Championships. Vivaldi won the Hamburg Jumping Derby three times. Baloubet du Rouet, considered to be one of the best show jumping horses of all time. Just some of the amazing horses founded and brought to top international success by Nelson Pessoa.

Nelson quickly became a legend in his home country of Brazil and also around the world. He opened the door for many other Brazilian riders who wanted to follow in his footsteps and became known as "The Wizard." He was also the winner of more than one hundred and fifty Grand Prix's in Europe and won more than one hundred Puissance competitions, he was also the Champion of Brazil on four different occasions.

Nelson is also in big demand as a coach of the sport and travels throughout Europe, the Middle East and Brazil. He assisted the Brazilian team to win a Bronze medal at the Atlanta Olympics, a first Show Jumping Gold Medal for them.

അ

However, Nelson considers his greatest achievement in coaching to be his son Rodrigo who is now a legend in his own lifetime including the 1998 World Championship and Olympic Gold Medallist.

Robert Trevor Banks

Michael Saywell riding Trevor Banks' Hideaway Munich 1972

Robert Trevor Banks was born in Yorkshire in 1929 and was raised in the Hull area of Yorkshire; his father was in the fish trade. Trevor started riding at an early age and won his first competitive trophy at the age of six. He eventually became the owner and dealer of many of the greatest horses to come out of Great Britain and had many of Britain's top International riders compete for him.

They included Harvey Smith, Mike Saywell, Malcolm Pyrah, Graham Fletcher and Captain Mark Phillips. He brought out many top show jumping and Three-Day Event horses of which many represented Great Britain around the world on various equestrian teams. He found Goodwill for H.R.H. Princess Anne and they represented Great Britain at the Montreal Olympics in Three-Day Eventing. Trevor was a large man and most definitely the typical outspoken Yorkshire man and was a familiar face at all of the major British shows and many abroad. Fate takes many paths in the lives of us all and it certainly took one for Malcolm Pyrah, a former stable jockey of Trevor's. Trevor loved to search out and buy horses, sometimes snapping them up under the noses of others and he had an incredible eye for a good horse. At the Horse of the Year Show Trevor watched a young rider, Adrian Marsh win the Calor Gas under twenty-one Championship in 1977 riding a horse called Anglezarke. Trevor wanted this horse badly, however, so did David Broome who apart from being one of the most famous show jumping riders in the world, was also a former World Champion. He bid against Trevor and eventually the price of the horse reached ninety thousand pounds, an unheard of sum in those days for a show jumping horse. Trevor paid the price and Adrian Marsh was able to buy his parents a farm with the proceeds.

CS

Trevor owned Anglezarke for two years and it looked like he would never get his large sum of money back on this horse.

He telephoned Malcolm Pyrah who at that time was competing with the British Team in Lucerne and asked Malcolm if his owners, Tom and Edna Hunnable would have any interest in buying Anglezark along with another horse he had, Chain Bridge. Chain Bridge had numerous successes with Michael Saywell including winning the King George V Gold Cup at the Royal International Horse Show in 1976. This was the horse that Malcolm and his sponsors, the Hunnables really were interested in buying. Later on, Chain Bridge would win the Dublin Grand Prix after which he slipped a tendon competing in Calgary and this unfortunately finished his career.

Anglezarke was offered at a much lower price than Trevor had paid for him to sweeten the deal and once Malcolm Pyrah started riding him, they clicked like crazy and together became one of the most successful British show jumping teams of all time. Apart from many National and International successes together, they also won Silver Medals in the World and European Championships. Another great horse that became a household name under the ownership of Trevor was Hideaway. Mark Phillips rode Hideaway as well as Michael Saywell and Hideaway competed in Nations Cups as well as two Olympic Games, in Munich with Mike in 1972 and four years later with Graham Fletcher in Montreal.

Trevor was a shrewd businessman and in 1977 when Sir Hugh Fraser, the owner of Harrods decided to quit the sport, Trevor bought all ten horses that Lady Aileen Fraser, the former Aileen Ross used to ride for one Hundred Thousand Pounds. This included a half share in another great horse, the grey, Bouncer half owned and ridden by Judy Crago. Bouncer competed with the British Show Jumping team at the Montreal Olympics ridden by Rowland Fernyhough, they were fourth in the individual competition just missing a Bronze Medal.

Trevor was also a British Show Jumping Association Judge, served on the B.S.J.A. Executive Committee and was involved in the sport of shooting which he loved for fun, he was a good shot so I was told. Trevor died on December 6th, 2002 at his home, Dalegate House, Bishop Burton, Beverley, North Humberside, he was 73.

Piero and Raimondo D'Inzeo

Major Raimondo and Piero D'Inzeo

Piero and Raimondo are the most famous brothers in the history of any sport in Italy and were the backbone for many years of the Italian Show Jumping Team. Piero is the oldest and was born in Rome on March 4th, 1923 eventually becoming a Colonel in the Italian Cavalry.

❧

Raimondo was born in Poggio Mireto on February 2nd, 1925 and became a Major.

Piero was the winner of six Olympic Medals and Raimondo was the winner of four. Together, they represented Italy all over the world and the two became Household names all of Europe. Throughout the sixties and seventies, they were incredibly popular in Great Britain competing at all of the major shows including the Horse of the Year Show, Royal International and of course, the Dublin Horse Show in Ireland. At the Dublin Horse Show, Piero won the Grand Prix in 1962 and Raimondo won it in 1969, they always seemed to follow in each other's footsteps. These are some of the highlights of Piero's career; I will start off with his four Olympic wins, 1956 in Stockholm, Silver medal in the team jumping and Individual Bronze riding Uruquay. 1960 in Rome, Bronze Medal Team and an Individual Silver riding The Rock. 1964 Tokyo, team bronze riding Sun Beam and at the 1972 Games in Munich, team Bronze riding Easter Light. Piero also had a wonderful record in the European Championships winning four individual medals throughout his career. 1958 in Aachen was the Individual Silver Medal winner riding The Rock. 1959 in Paris won the Individual Gold Medal on Uruquay. 1961 in Aachen won the Individual silver again on The Rock and in 1962 the Individual Bronze again on The Rock. He won man International Grand Prix's throughout his career including Aachen four times on different horses, one on Uruquay, once on Bally Black and twice on The Rock.

Piero Won the Grand Prix of Rome no less than seven times on different mounts, once on The Rock, twice on Sunbeam, once on Navarette, once on Fidux, once on Red Fox and twice on Easter Light. He also won the Grand Prix's of Amsterdam and Dublin. Raimondo had amazing success in his own right and won six Olympic Medals. In 1956 in Stockholm he won the team Silver and the Individual Silver riding Merano. 1960 in Rome, team Bronze and the Individual Gold riding Posillipo. 1964 in Tokyo a team Bronze riding Posillipo and in Munich another team Bronze Medal; riding Fiorello II. He had a wonderful record in the World Championships starting off in 1955 with an Individual Silver Medal riding Merano in Aachen. In 1956, also riding Merano, they won the Individual Gold Medal, also in Aachen. 1960 he won the Gold Medal again in Venice riding Gowran Girl and in 1966 won the Individual Bronze riding Bowjak. Raimondo also won the Rome Grand Prix on four occasions, first in 1956 and 57 riding Merano then in 1971 on Fiorello then again in 1974 aboard Gone Away. What can one say about these two amazing Italian brothers that has not been said already? They both truly represented the Golden Age of Show Jumping with absolute flying colors. Not just representing with constant

164

honors their country Italy, but between them individually winning every show jumping title imaginable on many different horses.

CB

Raimondo was Olympic Champion and double World Champion. Together with his elder brother Piero D'Inzeo, they were the first athletes, to compete in eight Olympic Games, extremely consistently from 1948 to 1976. Their most amazing achievement together was at the Olympic Games in 1960, in Rome, when Raimondo won the gold medal and Piero won the silver in the Olympic show jumping final. Throughout Italy, they were known as the brothers invincible and are still revered in Italy as two of the greatest athletes ever.

The picture on the preceding pages is an incredible and rare photograph indeed of these two iconic legends of our sport and historical heroes of Italy and winners all around the world in International Show Jumping. This includes Raimondo winning the Olympic Gold Medal and Piero winning the Silver on home turf at the 1960 Rome Summer Olympic Games. Brother's making a nation proud standing side by side on an Olympic Podium.

Sadly, we lost both of these amazing ambassadors to the sport over the past three months. Raimondo passed away in November of last year and Piero just a couple of weeks ago on February 13th. Piero was the oldest and I believe could not go on without his brother at his side. They were almost inseparable and always together since childhood.

Being both Military men, they were always turned out to perfection in their uniforms and this is how they competed their whole careers.

R.I.P. Major Raimondo and Colonel Piero D'Inzeo, you will never be forgotten in the history of the Golden Age of Show Jumping!

Anneli Drummond-Hay

Anneli Drummond-Hay and the amazing Merely-a-Monarch.

Anneli and "Monarch" as he was affectionately known are the only combination of horse and rider to compete at the highest level in Eventing, Dressage and Show Jumping. Together, they held numerous titles throughout their illustrious career.

When Anneli was just sixteen years old she won the Pony Club European Championships. She then found her wonderful partner Merely-a-Monarch and together they won Burghley and Badminton, at Badminton they headed into the record books winning by the largest margin in history.

Then Anneli decided to compete in Show Jumping with Monarch and together they won everything including the Ladies European Championship and the Queen Elizabeth II Cup. Anneli too Monarch to the United States and competed at Madison Square Garden in New York and the Washington National Horse Show in Washington D.C. Her teammate on that trip was Althea Roger-Smith with Havanah Royal. Anneli and Monarch's wins together are far too numerous to mention. They were also members of the Nations Cup winning teams in London, Rome and Geneva. In Rome and Geneva, she was the leading lady rider. Anneli also rode O'Malley's Tango and Xanthos winning the British Jumping Derby on Xanthos at Hickstead.

℃℥

Merely-a-Monarch was voted as one of the best fifty horses of the last century having made an enormous name for himself in all disciplines. He was only six years old when he won the Burghley Horse Trials and just one year later he and Anneli won Badminton. That same year, they won many Grand Prix's in Show Jumping and were short listed for the 1964 Olympics in Tokyo. Monarch also was a top class Dressage Horse and Rosemary Springer, the five time German Olympian tried to buy him for Dressage. Later in his life, he was actually short listed for the British Senior Dressage Team. In 1995 Monarch was inducted into the BHS Hall of Fame. Anneli is still going strong and competing in South Africa running Penny Place Stables. I have had a crush on her all my life, ever since I danced with her when I was thirteen years old.

This was at the Southport Show Dinner Dance back in the sixties. I was about thirteen years old and she was sitting at the table with Harvey Smith and David Broome, I asked her to dance and she said yes. She made a young, besotted boy very happy that night and I have not forgotten, nor will I ever forget, how delightful she was. Later in life when I started commentating, Anneli and I became friends and it was a great loss to British Show Jumping when she moved to South Africa.

Throughout his career Merely-A-Monarch was taken care of by Anneli's groom and friend, Merlin Meakin who looked after him well into his retirement. Merlin was a successful Three Day Event rider in her own right.

Ted Edgar

Ted Edgar on Uncle Max

Ted Edgar was born in 1935 and throughout the late fifties and the sixties was a member of the British Show Jumping team with a horse called Jane Summers. A little chestnut mare that was a super horse for Ted and together they competed at all of the shows throughout the U.K. including wins at the Horse of the Year Show and the Royal International. Ted really made the headlines in the seventies when he came to the show jumping arena with Uncle Max. The feisty, acrobatic Uncle Max was a horse that Ted bought from Neal Shapiro in the United States.

‘’

Together they excited crowds wherever they competed and eventually won the coveted King George V Gold cup at the Royal International Horse Show in 1969. The trophy that night was presented to a very proud Ted by Her Majesty the Queen.

Ted married Elizabeth Broome the sister of David Broome and we all affectionately called her Liz Edgar. Ted took a role away from the competition side of show jumping and became a full time dealer and trainer. He and his wife Liz formed the Everest Stud and joined forces with the Everest Double Glazing Company as their major sponsor. Together, Ted and Liz took on a very promising young rider by the name of Nick Skelton who for several years rode under the Everest name and won all over Europe including setting a new high jump record at Olympia on Everest Lastic jumping more than seven feet six inches in 1978.

Ted can still be seen around the Show Jumping circuit and is always watching taking in everything with a great eye for a good horse and is always encouraging to the young riders of today. A man with a wealth of knowledge of the Show Jumping world and one who has become a great ambassador to the sport. He with Liz now train their daughter Marie Edgar who has become one of the top young riders in Britain and has certainly followed in the International footsteps of her parents Ted and Liz Edgar.

❀

Ted Edgar and Uncle Max Pictured here - They won the King George V Gold Cup at the Royal International Horse Show. The Horse came from Neal Shapiro in the United States and was an ex Rodeo horse.

John and Jane Kidd

John and Jane Kidd and their mother The Honorable Mrs. Edward Kidd

In the late sixties, early seventies I worked and rode for their mother, the late Hon. Mrs. Edward Kidd, (Janet). She owned the Maple Stud in Ewhurst, Surrey and was a successful equestrian in her own right. Mrs. Kidd was the breeder of Fjord ponies and had an amazing International Driving career and was known throughout the world in this discipline.

The first time Mrs. Kidd competed was at Hickstead in 1974. Rachael Carpenter, her navigator and companion was amazing and at the end of the three-day competition had helped Mrs. Kidd win the Championship. Pretty amazing for their first time out together beating some of the most experienced Driving teams in the sport. They went on to win the National Championship, The Pitney Bowes at the Royal International Horse Show and the British Driving Derby. Before she started driving competitively with the Fjord's, she operated a breeding stud of Hanoverian horses producing some successful show jumping horses in Great Britain. Mrs. Kidd retired in 1985 and passed away in 1988 at age 80, three years after she retired from competition as one of the most successful Fjord Driving competitors in history. Mrs. Kidd formed the Barbados Show Jumping Federation in the 1960's and introduced many forms of equestrianism to the island.

By then, John was an established International Show Jumping rider and had competed on such horses as Copper Castle, Mill Street, Bali Hai, Sam Lord and when I joined them was riding Grey Owl. Grey Owl was a former horse of his sister Jane and after a riding accident when she broke her back, Johnny as he was known, took over the ride. When Jane recovered, she then took up Dressage as her back did not allow her to go back to Show Jumping.

ᚠ

The family have a home on the island of Barbados and have brought a variety of equestrian events there including Polo of which Johnny competed extensively in after he gave up show jumping. His daughters and many members of his family have also become involved with the sport of Polo.

Their family is steeped in British history with Mrs. Kidd, born in 1908 former Duchess of Argyll their mother who was the daughter of Lord Beaverbrook. Lord Beaverbrook managed for almost a year to keep the story of Edward and Mrs. Simpson out of the British newspapers and he was a great friend of the King. He held a very tight grip on British Media and was the owner of The Daily Express, Sunday Express and the London Evening Standard.

Johnny Kidd on Grey Owl

Johnny represented Great Britain throughout Europe and in the United States and had many wins nationally including coming second to the great Hans Gunter Winkler at the Horse of the Year Show. He also rode with the British Team in France and was second in La Baule with Grey Owl. Johnny is the father of world famous model and T.V. personality Jodie Kidd. Johnny's elder daughter is Jemma Kidd who married Arthur Gerald Wellesley, Earl of Mornington, he is the grandson of the Duke of Wellington.

Kevin Bacon

Kevin Bacon riding Chichester showing his distinct and unique style of riding, was taken by Ghislaine Mathieu.

Kevin Ashley Bacon was born in Dungog, New South Wales, Australia on March 20th 1932 and grew up to become a three-time Olympian Show Jumper. His first Olympics was in the 1964 Tokyo Games with team mates Thomas Fahey and Bridget MacIntyre. Kevin rode a horse called Ocean Foam. He then represented Australia at the 1968 Olympics in Mexico City with his teammates John Fahey and Sam Campbell. Kevin's final Olympics was in Montreal, Canada in 1976 riding his great little horse, Chichester. He was joined by Guy Creighton and Barry Roycroft. Kevin was also a four-time champion at Madison Square Garden in New York and also won Grand Prix's in Canada and Europe. He also won the Berlin International Championship on his great little Chichester. Kevin had an incredibly unique jumping style and when he jumped his body and legs were completely out of the saddle, much like Alan Oliver used to ride. You absolutely saw daylight between Kevin and the horse when they jumped. Kevin is only five feet six and weighed in at one hundred and forty-six pounds.

Kevin definitely had a different way of riding and it was many times describes as 'determined' rather than one of style. In fact, at the first American and European shows, the audiences would laugh at Kevin as he rode around the arena, however, after big wins in New York, Toronto and other major shows the laughter soon turned to one of applause and admiration. His little Jet Black Chichester also had an unusual show jumping style and became one of the favorites worldwide of show jumping fans.

On November 2nd, 2000, Kevin was awarded the Australian Sports Medal for his services and achievements to the world of Equestrianism. He now lives in Europe coaching and training so he is still very much a part of the Equestrian World that he loves.

Caroline Bradley

Caroline Bradley and Milton

Caroline Bradley brought Milton out as a novice before she tragically died. Gone too soon, Caroline, you will never be forgotten, not as long as I am around, I was so lucky to have known you and called you a friend. Caroline rode a great stallion called Marius, he was the sire of Milton. She knew when he was a baby that Milton would be one of the greatest of all time, and he was, becoming the first show jumper to win a million pounds with John Whitaker.

Foaled in 1977, Milton was by Dutch Warmblood Marius, out of Irish Draught Aston Answers. His lines included successful sports horses in both paternal and maternal lines, his sire being an international level and his dam a Grade A national level jumper.

When Milton was young, Caroline Bradley told her parents he would be her Olympic mount. She trained him until her death in 1983, after which many offers were made to her parents to buy the gelding, who had already proven his talent. They kept the horse.

Stephen Hadley, known later as a FEI TV show jumping commentator, rode Milton for a short time, before he became a mount of the world-renowned international rider John Whitaker. Milton entered inter-national competition in 1985.

During his competitive career, Milton achieved many international victories, and became the first horse outside the racing world to win more than £1 million in prize money. Throughout his career, Milton rarely touched a rail or refused a fence. The gelding was a favorite with the crowd, many times ending a successful round with a leap into the air. Even after his retirement at the 1994 Olympia Horse Show, he was adored by all. Milton died on 4 July 1999. He was buried on the Whitaker's farm in Yorkshire, a farm I used to visit often to spend time with the Whitaker's in the 70's.

C3

Caroline won the Queen Elizabeth II Cup twice, the Toronto Open Show Jumping Championship and was the second woman to win the Hamburg Jumping Derby. Caroline's best horses were Tigre and Marius. In 1979 she was voted Daily Express Sportswoman of the Year. At her peak, Caroline was ranked by many as the greatest lady rider in the world, and in the eyes of many experts, she was. Tragedy struck at the Ipswich show on June 1st, 1983 when Caroline collapsed and attempts to revive her where to no avail. H.R.H. Princess Margaret was the guest of honor at the show and was shocked at Caroline's death. In 1980 H.M. Queen Elizabeth bestowed upon Caroline the Member of the Order of the British Empire.

Gone too soon dear Caroline, R.I.P.

Stephen Hadley

The Great Milton with Stephen Hadley

Here is a super photograph of Stephen aboard Milton at the Newbury show, 1983 in the days before the ride was given to John Whitaker. John and Milton's partnership is one of the greatest ever in the history of Show Jumping.

What many do not know is that for a short while after we tragically lost Caroline Bradley, International rider Stephen Hadley rode Milton for Caroline's parents.

❧

Stephen was known for his winnings aboard Flying Wild and others and eventually became one of the voices of Show Jumping when he became a commentator after I had left England.

Seamus Hayes

Seamus Hayes and Goodbye - Ireland

What an amazing and illustrious career this combination had as well as being the very first ever horse and rider to win the Hickstead Jumping Derby together in 1961. They came back three years later winning again in 1964.

Seamus and Goodbye were always at the big shows in London, especially the Horse of the Year Show and the Royal International Horse Show.

∝

At these events and many throughout the world they would take top honors and go back to Ireland with their share of trophies, ribbons and prizes. They also represented Ireland on many occasions as a Nations Cup team member and also helped them win the Aga Khan Trophy several times.

Seamus led the way for Ireland with Iris Kellet and Tommy Wade and opened the door in the sport for other great Irish Riders. These included Tommy Brennan, Patrick Connolly Carew and his sister The Hon. Diana Connolly Carew, Ned Campion, Paul Darragh and many others leading to probably the best ever out of Ireland, Eddie Macken and Boomerang.

These riders and many more added to the excitement, glamour and stardom of the horses and riders of the Golden Age of Show Jumping.

The picture above is a rare photograph of Seamus riding Goodbye at the Royal Dublin Horse Show. This photograph is courtesy of Irish Life.

Marion Mould (Coakes)

The great Stroller and Marion Mould (Coakes)

Stroller (1950-1986) was the only pony to compete at the Olympics in Show Jumping. He was even more of a marvel because he was just 14.1 hh and in his heart, he absolutely believed he was a horse. Stroller was a Bay Gelding with a star on his forehead, a Thoroughbred cross Connemara and was owned and ridden my Marion Mould (the former Marion Coakes) from Hampshire, England. Marion's father Ralph Coakes bought Stroller in Ireland in 1960, Marion was just thirteen years old at the time and somehow knew that this was a partnership that would last a lifetime.

Even though he was a pony, Marion decided that he had the heart of a horse and in her mind believed he was one. She refused to part with him and together they went on to be two of the most successful combinations of horse and rider in history, or should I say pony and rider?

He was a member of the British team who competed in the 1968 Olympics in Mexico, ridden by Marion Coakes. Bill Steinkraus and Snowbound won the Gold Medal while Marion and Stroller won the Individual Silver Medal, only four faults behind Steinkraus. Stroller jumped one of the only two clear rounds in the Olympic individual championship.

In 1964 and 1967, Marion rode 14.1 hh Stroller to victory in the Hickstead Derby, the only pony to have ever won this world class coveted event. This partnership won the Wills Hickstead Gold Medal, for points gained in the major events during the year, for five years consecutively from 1965 to 1970. Stroller was the grand age of 20 when he won the 1970 Hamburg Derby. The pair won 61 international competitions. They also helped Great Britain win many Nations Cups also was on the winning British team that won the Presidents Cup. Together in 1965 they also won the Ladies World Championship at Hickstead. They also won the Leading Show Jumper of the Year title at the Horse of the Year Show a Wembley.

 CB

Stroller died of a heart attack at the high age 36 in 1986, after 15 years of happy retirement. He is buried at Barton-on-Sea Golf Club, New Milton, Hampshire, England.

CB

Individual Silver medal at the 1968 Olympic Games (Mexico)

Winner of the Women's Show Jumping World Championships 1965 (Hickstead)

Won 1967 Hickstead Derby

Won 1970 Hamburg Derby (as only clear round) Winner of the Queen Elizabeth II Cup 1965 and 1971

2nd place, Women's World Championships 1970 (Copenhagen)

Only pony to compete at International level among horses and win consistently in Europe

BHS (British Horse Society) Hall of Fame Laureate

႓

After Stroller, Marion rode several other horses with some success including Daddy's Girl and Elizabeth Ann, sponsored by Elizabeth Ann Kitchens. After she had retired Stroller in 1971 she had some successes including winning the Queen Elizabeth II Cup again in 1975, however, Marion never reached the kind of success again that she had with the one of a kind, Stroller. He and Marion truly became two of the most famous stars of the Golden Age of Show Jumping. Marion married the Steeplechase Jockey David Mould in 1969 who was rider of many horses owned by Queen Elizabeth the Queen Mother.

They have a son Jack who now plays football for a team in Spain. They go back and forth between Spain and their home in Hampshire.

Graziano Mancinelli

Graziano Mancinelli on Ambassador in Munich

Graziano Mancinelli was born in Milan, Italy on February 18th 1937. He became one of the most famous Italian Show Jumpers of all time and often rode beside the D'Inzeo brothers.

Graziano celebrated most of his success in the 1960's and 1970's including riding in the Olympic Games, World and European Championships. In 1972 he won the individual Olympic Gold Medal riding his Irish bred Gelding Ambassador in Munich.

He was also a member of the Italian Olympic team in Tokyo where they won the Team Bronze Medal. Graziano competed in the World Championship in La Baule, 1970 bringing home the Individual Silver and won the Individual Gold Medal at the European Championships in Rome riding Rockeette, 1963. Graziano was the National Champion of

Italy on no less than six occasions. He passed away on 8 October 1992 in Concesio.

Pictured above Graziano Mancinelli - Ambassador - Gold for Italy. Ann Moore - Psalm - Silver for Great Britain. Neal Shapiro - Sloopy - Bronze United States of America.

Hans Gunter Winkler

Hans was probably the greatest rider to ever come out of Germany having had International, World Championship and Olympic success on many different horses. Hans was born on July 24th, 1926 in Barmen, Germany and started riding at a very early age becoming one of the greatest riders the world had ever seen. It is hard to believe that throughout his career he won five Olympic Gold Medals, the only Show Jumper to ever achieve this feat. He won a total of seven Olympic medals in all winning in six different Olympic Games.

⋈

In the 1950's and 1960's, Hans Winkler became Germany's most popular athlete winning he first German Championship in 1952, which was an Olympic year with the summer games being held in Helsinki, Finland. Of course, this win immediately put him in the funning as one of the favorites for the 1956 Olympics in Stockholm. Of course, he was selected to represent Germany on the show jumping team and severely pulled a groin muscle when Halla jumped a little early throwing him out of position in the saddle. He was in tremendous pain, however, decided to jump in the third round owing to the fact that the German team would be eliminated if he did not compete. The doctors gave him tranquilizers and though Hans was comfortable sitting in the saddle, it was very difficult and painful to actual ride, especially jump. Even though the painkillers would have helped him a little in the saddle with the groin pull, his mental capacity would have been reduced owing to the effects of the medication. So the only thing he was given to help reduce the dizziness and double vision was black coffee. His unbelievable mare and ride that day, Halla seemed to sense that Hans was not right and jumped the entire course clear without any real riding from Hans; this incredible faultless round gave them the Individual Gold Medal.

Cи

Hans and Halla became immediate Olympic hero's adding this to the back-to-back World Championships they had already won before arriving in Stockholm. Four years after this unbelievable achievement, Hans and Halla led the German team to another victory at the Olympic Games in Rome.

Halla was most definitely one of the greatest Show Jumping horse in history and with Hans won three Olympic Gold Medals. She was 16.2 hh. She died at the age of 34 on May 19th 1979. After retiring from the sport of Show Jumping, Halla actually had eight foals, though none of them even came close to becoming the incredible Champion that their mother had been throughout her career. Hans and Halla won a total of one hundred and twenty-five show jumping competitions together and still hold the record in the Guinness Book of Records as the horse with the most Olympic Gold Medals.

Despite the pain, Winkler decided to ride in the third round, as the German team would be eliminated without him. After he was given tranquilizers, Winkler found that he was comfortable sitting, but riding was difficult and painful. Any drugs that could reduce the pain enough to make him comfortable in the saddle would also reduce his mental capacity, and therefore he was only given black coffee before his ride to try to help reduce his dizziness and double vision. However, his great mare, Halla, sensed that her rider was not right, and performed the entire course clear with only steering from Winkler, and their performance won them the individual gold.

Winkler won five gold medals in jumping (in addition to the four individual medals with the German team) between 1956 and 1976, and a silver medal. He is one of the most successful German Olympic athletes, second only to the great Reiner Klimke for gold medals produced in German equestrian competition. He was 1955 and 1956 to athlete of the year. In 1986, Winkler retired from active competition. He has since published numerous books on riding and founded in 1991 the HGW-Marketinggesellschaft, a sports marketing firm that has helped produce various equestrian competitions. He is also a member of the German Equestrian Federation's Jumping Committee, and helped to select the 2000 Olympic Team for Germany.

Paddy McMahon

Paddy McMahon and the great Penwood Forge Mill

Patrick "Paddy" McMahon was born on December 5th, 1933 in Derby, England and it was in the stars that he was to become a star, one of the biggest stars of top International Show Jumping.

I am honored indeed to call one of the greatest Show Jumpers of all time my dear friend, the great Paddy McMahon. Penwood Forge Mill and Paddy were hugely popular during the time of their career and still remain one of Britain's best-loved Show Jumping combinations.

Their early successes included winning the Grand Prix in Ostend and coming second in the Nations Cup competitions at Ostend, Rotterdam and Geneva, both in 1971. In the following year, together they came second in the Nations Cup in Rome, before achieving a first in London. They then went on to win back-to-back Nations Cups in 1977 and 1978.

One of the most exciting competitions ever which was televised was the night Paddy and Forgie were last to go in the Victor Ludorum at the Horse of the Year Show. I will never forget that night, I was sitting in the commentary box at Wembley with the great Dorian Williams, Paddy and Forgie were the last to go and Paul Schockermohle was in the lead. There were eighteen thousand people in the audience that night and as Paddy and Forgie set off one could have heard a pin drop. As they galloped around the arena against the clock, the crowd starting off with a murmur, it then got louder and as Paddy and Forgie came down the last line of fences people were already coming to their feet. As Paddy and Forgie shot through the finish the winners in 28.3 seconds eighteen thousand people raised the roof off the Empire Pool that night. Dorian had tears coming down his face, I was choked up and it was impossible to announce that he was clear in the fastest time, the winners. Obviously, none of those at Wembley that night needed to be told because those eighteen thousand people and the millions watching at home on television already knew.

ೞ

It was one of the magical moments of the Golden Age of Show Jumping, a night never to be forgotten. When I told Paddy about all of our responses in the commentary booth including the tears on Dorian's face, he got quite emotional and said, "Ohhhhh Frank, what a wonderful memory."

Incredibly, Paddy and Forgie as he was affectionately known also won the European Championships at Hickstead in 1973 beating the great German rider, Alwin Schockermohle. They then together won the King George V Gold Cup and the Horse and Hound Cup within six days! An amazing feat and probably a record to this day. When they won he King George V Gold Cup, Paddy, Forgie and Forgie's owner Fred Harthill were presented to H.M. the Queen who awarded them with the trophy, one of the highlights of Paddy's life, a moment he will never forget. That same year Paddy was voted into third place for the B.B.C. Sports Personality of the Year Award.

Paddy thank you so much, for being who you are and for supporting this book as you have. You are certainly one of the main characters who made show jumping what it was in the Golden era. You brought so many to the edge of their seats with your amazing jump off skills culminating in becoming the Men's European Champion in 1973 at Hickstead. Paddy, Harvey, David, Marion, Anneli and so many others brought the excitement of this sport into all of our living rooms and made show jumping in Britain as famous as football and horse racing.

Many of those Horses and Riders today are still household names and will never be forgotten and my goal is to bring you all back into those living rooms through my book "The Golden Age of Show Jumping."

Paul Schockemöhle

Paul Schockemöhle and Diester

Paul was born on March 22nd 1945 in Muhlen, Oldenburg, Germany and with his brother Alwin grew up to be two of the greatest Show Jumping riders ever to come out of that nation.

છ

Paul won the European Championship on no less than three occasions on his great horse Deister. Some of the most famous wins of Paul include the 1976 Team Silver at the Montreal Olympics with Agent. The 1981 team Gold and Individual Gold Medal at the European Championships in Munich riding Deister.

Again, in 1983 he won the Individual Gold Medal at the European Championships at Hickstead once more riding Deister. With Deister, together they helped Germany win the Team Bronze at the Los Angeles Olympic Games. The following year, 1985 he and Deister won the Individual Gold Medal and the Team Bronze at the European Championships held in Dinard, once again riding his great horse Deister.

Paul also won the Hickstead Derby three times, in 1982 riding Deister, in 1985 riding Lorenzo and in 1986 once again with the great Deister.

What an unbelievable combination of horse and rider, Germany's Paul Schockermohle and Deister. Together they broke many records including winning three consecutive European Show Jumping Gold Medals. The first together was in Munich, Germany in 1981, then at Hickstead in 1983 followed by their third win in Dinard, France in 1985.

However, they did win their first European Medal together in 1979 at Rotterdam when they won the Silver behind Gerd Wiltfang riding Roman also for Germany. Deister was an extraordinary Bay Hanno-varian Gelding by Diskant out of Adlerklette.

CB

Part of his amazing career brought him the German Championship on five occasions and winner of the Aachen Grand Prix in 1984. In 1983, they won the King George V Gold Cup at Hickstead and also the Hickstead Derby in 1982 and 1986. Despite his amazing career the hardy Deister, who was born in February 1971, lived to the ripe old age of 29.

Alwin Schockemöhle

Alwin Schockemöhle on Warwick Rex

Alwin was one of the greatest Show Jumping riders ever and was also one of the most beautiful and stylish riders to watch.

ଔ

I learned a lot as a young rider watching him both live and on television and I always wanted to ride just like him. He was the epitome of class and still is respected throughout the world for his skills and expertise.

Alwin was born on May 29th in Meppen near Hanover in Germany. Most of his success came in the 1960's and 70's; including individual and team appearances in Olympic Games and European

191

Championships. He won his first Olympic Gold Medal at the 1960 Games in Rome while representing the German Team and one the Bronze in 1968 at the Mexico City Olympics.

Captain Con Power

Many have asked me about Con Power who was one of the top International Riders out of the great Equestrian country, Ireland. He is very much involved still in the sport and coaches many youngsters. Con's daughter Liz competes in Three Day Eventing for Ireland.

Here is Con recently presenting a very proud Eoin Cleare as winner of the "Paralympic Sports Award" at this year's RCTLC Sports awards. Con was the guest of honor and made all at this awards ceremony proud indeed to be in his company.

Graham Fletcher

Graham Fletcher and Buttevant Boy at Hickstead

Graham was one of the top International Show Jumping riders for Great Britain and competed for more than thirty years.

His successes include an Olympic Silver Medal, three times an Olympic team member, twice British National Champion and Leading Show Jumper of the Year to name a few. I first saw Graham when he was 16 riding Buttevant Boy in the Foxhunter Final at Wembley, they were fourth, Buttevant Boy was only four at the time and they eventually went on to win the Young Riders Calor Gas Championship. The rest of their illustrious career together is part of Show Jumping history. Amongst many of his other top horses was Tauna Dora and Hideaway for Trevor Banks.

Col. Harry Llewellyn

Col. Harry Llewellyn and Foxhunter

Sir Harry Morton Llewellyn, 3rd Baronet, CBE was born on July 18th, 1911 in Aberdare, South Wales and was the son of a colliery owner, Sir David Llewelly, 1st Baronet. Harry inherited the Baronetcy in 1978 after his younger brother Sir David Llewellyn died, David was a Conservative politician. Harry was educated at Oundle School and Trinity College Cambridge and eventually joined the Army. A very interesting bit of history on Harry which many readers will find fascinating, Harry had some success in Show Jumping in the 1930's, however, he also competed in the Grand National in 1936 and came second.

ೞ

During World War II, Harry was stationed in Italy and after D Day in Normandy served as liaison Officer to Field Marshal Montgomery and eventually rose through the ranks of become a Colonel of the British Army.

After the war Harry Llewellyn concentrated on show jumping, buying Foxhunter in 1947 after an incredibly long search for the right horse. Together, they went on to be part of the British Show Jumping Team that won a bronze medal in the team event at the 1948 Summer Olympics in London.

They then captured the adoration of the British and world equestrian crowds for their role in winning Great Britain's only gold medal at the 1952 Summer Olympics, in the Team Show Jumping.

Harry Llewellyn and Foxhunter won 78 International competitions during their career together. Harry later served widely in the administration of British show jumping, and was knighted in 1977 before inheriting the Llewellyn Baronetcy upon the death of his brother. Sir Harry had many business interests including brewing and television. After winning Team Gold at the 1952 Olympics in Helsinki, he founded a chain of cafes named after his great partner in show jumping, Foxhunter. Sir Harry was inducted into the Welsh Sports Hall of Fame in 1990. He was married to Christine Saumarz, the daughter of the fifth Baron de Saumares.

ॐ

They had two sons, Dai and Roddy who became celebrities in their own right including a long time affair between Roddy and H.R.H. Princess Margaret.

When Harry Llewellyn died on November 15th, 1999, his ashes were scattered near Foxhunter's grave and memorial on Blorenge Mountain above Abergavenny in Wales.

Harry was a true pioneer of our sport and certainly legends of the Golden Age of Show Jumping.

Andrew Fielder

Andrew Fielder and the unique kick backing Vibart.

My good friend of more than fifty years. Andrew Fielder on Vibart. Andrew and Vibart won the leading show jumper of the year when he was only sixteen. I believe that record still stands today. Vibart always stunned the crowds and they constantly gasped at his massive kick back when he jumped.

I was there that night at Wembley and will never forget Jack, Andrew's dad picking me up and throwing me in the air shouting; "He's done it, he's done it" he was so excited. That was the real start of an amazing career for Andrew and Bart, as he was known. He was on many British teams including being short-listed for the Olympics.

Those were incredible days in our spot, so many characters and personalities, riders and horses, which we do not see today. I was so fortunate to have been a part of the magnificent "Golden Age of Show Jumping."

Frank Waters pictured here with Dorian Williams when they were commentating at The Horse of the Year Show Wembley

Team Great Britain. David Broome on Heatwave, Harvey Smith on Salvador, Paddy McMahon on Penwood Forgemill and Graham

Fletcher on Tauna Dora, Hickstead in 1975, truly The Golden Age of Show Jumping

Frank Waters (Left) with John Whitaker and Ryan's Son back in the seventies at Wembley. I am talking with Claire, his now wife. Graham Fletcher and Tony Newberry in the background. At Wembley, London, England 1978

Frank Waters

Andrew Fielder and I in Tenerife, Canary Islands

Back in 1974 before Andrew married the love of his life, Maddy Bowey, he and I decided to have a holiday in the Canary Islands. This was February, very cold in England and we left his house at Pool in Wharfedale, Yorkshire in the middle of the night and headed for Gatwick Airport, south of London.

ᏨᏋ

I remember the drive in Andrew's car, a purple sporty Avenger and we played the Carpenter's on the cassette deck, actually, it may have been an eight track, we did not have CD players then. On arrival at Gatwick, we boarded a British Caledonian VC10 aircraft. A wonderfully quiet plane with two engines set either side of the aircraft below the tail. Wonderful service, charming flight attendants all part of a time gone by like the Golden Age of Show Jumping.

We had a fun week with lots of laughs and super sunny warm weather. However, Andrew missed Maddy terribly and called her daily, God knows what his phone bill was in those days as it was done from the telephone in the room, no Cell Phones in those days.

Andrew and Maddy married on July 21st, 1974 and are still very happy together, Vibart was one of the guests of honor at the wedding. Andrew and Maddy are now very proud grandparents and live in the Newcastle area, he now rides Dressage!

Above is a photograph of Andrew and I in one of the Tenerife Bar's, how young we were, we even had hair! What wonderful memories of The Golden Age of Show Jumping, sadly, never to be repeated!

All England Jumping Course, Hickstead, Bolney, Sussex

The All England Jumping course was opened by Douglas Bunn, former barrister who made his money as the owner of caravan parks in the south of England. Duggie opened the AEJC in 1960 and started receiving support from top British and European Riders almost immediately. He bought a piece of property known as Hickstead Place with the intention of creating a World Class Show Jumping venue and his dream was to make it the best in the world. After he opened The All England Jumping Course, it quickly became known throughout the world as just Hickstead. It is located on the main A23 road which is the main road from London to Brighton in the actual village of Hickstead.

It now has six arenas, permanent seating for more than 5,000 spectators and 26 corporate hospitality suites. Hickstead hosted the 1965 Ladies World Championships, the 1974 World Championships and several European Show Jumping Championships. It is also the home of the British Jumping Derby and Longines Royal International Horse Show. The first major sponsor that Duggie brought in that was part of Hickstead for many years was W.D. & H.O Wills. It has now become one of the premier show grounds for Dressage and fittingly now has the British Dressage Derby as well as hosting Polo. It set the standard of becoming the first permanent show ground in the United Kingdom. It has now grown into Douglas Bunn's dream as one of the finest show grounds in the world and apart from the British Jumping Derby and the RIHS it also hosts many social activities throughout the year including weddings, birthday parties and other social activities.

I have to say, that the highlight of the calendar year at Hickstead has to be the British Jumping Derby. It is 1,195 meters long and has some of the most difficult fences in Show Jumping. This includes the Devil's Dyke consisting of three jumps in short succession and a water-filled ditch in the middle and of course the Derby Bank. The bank is approached from the back and once on top of this bank, which stands at 10 ft. 6 inches (3.20 m), they have to jump a 3 ft. 5 in rail, come to a halt and then slide down the bank with another jump directly in front of them.

Hickstead has permanent seating for more than five thousand spectators and twenty-six corporate hospitality suites.

Douglas Bunn's dream of becoming the best in the world has definitely come to fruition, thank you Dougie!

Here are the winners of the Hickstead Derby from the very beginning in 1961 to the present, 2013:

Year	Rider	Country	Horse
1961	Seamus Hayes	IRL	Goodbye III
1962	Pat Smythe	GBR	Flanagan
1963	Nelson Pessoa	BRA	Gran Geste
1964	Seamus Hayes	IRL	Goodbye III
1965	Nelson Pessoa	BRA	Gran Geste
1966	David Broome	GBR	Mister Softee
1967	Marion Coakes	GBR	Stroller
1968	Alison Westwood	GBR	The Maverick III
1969	Anneli Drummond-	GBR	Xanthos II

Hay

1970	Harvey Smith	GBR	Mattie Brown
1971	Harvey Smith	GBR	Mattie Brown
1972	Hendrik Snoek	GER	Shirokko
1973	Alison Dawes (Westwood)	GBR	Mr. Banbury
1974	Harvey Smith	GBR	Salvador
1975	Paul Darragh	IRL	Pele
1976	Eddie Macken	IRL	Boomerang
1977	Eddie Macken	IRL	Boomerang
1978	Eddie Macken	IRL	Boomerang
1979	Eddie Macken	IRL	Boomerang
1980	Michael Whitaker	GBR	Owen Gregory
1981	Harvey Smith	GBR	Sanyo Video
1982	Paul Schockemöhle	GER	Deister
1983	John Whitaker	GBR	Ryan's Son
1984	John Ledingham	IRL	Gabhran
1985	Paul Schockemöhle	GER	Lorenzo
1986	Paul Schockemöhle	GER	Deister
1987	Nick Skelton	GBR	J. Nick
1988	Nick Skelton	GBR	Apollo

1989	Nick Skelton	GBR	Apollo
1990	Jozsef Turi	GBR	Vital
1991	Michael Whitaker	GBR	Monsanta
1992	Michael Whitaker	GBR	Monsanta
1993	Michael Whitaker	GBR	Monsanta
1994	John Ledingham	IRL	Kilbaha
1995	John Ledingham	IRL	Kilbaha
1996	Nelson Pessoa	BRA	Loro Piana Vivaldi
1997	John Popely	GBR	Bluebird
1998	John Whitaker	GBR	Gammon
1999	Rob Hoekstra	GBR	Lionel II
2000	John Whitaker	GBR	Welham
2001	Peter Charles	IRL	Corrada
2002	Peter Charles	IRL	Corrada
2003	Peter Charles	IRL	Corrada
2004	John Whitaker	GBR	Buddy Bunn
2005	Ben Maher	GBR	Alfredo II
2006	William Funnell	GBR	Cortaflex Mondriaan
2007	Geoff Billington	GBR	Cassabachus
2008	William Funnell	GBR	Cortaflex Mondriaan
2009	William Funnell	GBR	Cortaflex Mondriaan

2010	Guy Williams	GBR	Skip Two Ramiro
2011	Tina Fletcher	GBR	Promised Land
2012	Paul Beecher	IRL	Loughnatousa WB
2013	Phillip Miller	GBR	Caritiar Z

Chapter Twenty-One

Rounding up
The Golden Age of Show Jumping
Volume 1

There were so many wonderful and unforgettable time on the road when we travelled the show jumping circuit. We were like a band of Gypsies really as we travelled the many country lanes of England in our Horseboxes with Caravans attached to the back.

With only the M1 and a shortened version of the M6, most of our driving was on rural roads. In those days our caravans did not have toilets or shower rooms and it became difficult sometimes to have a regular bath. At a lot of the showground's we would be in the Gents stripped to the waist with many of the riders and grooms. Sinks full of soapy water with face cloths or sponges washing ourselves the best we could and at the same time telling jokes, laughing at the silliest things but most of all making it fun. We never complained that was our lifestyle and when we did arrive at a show that had showering or bathing facilities, it was an absolute luxury.

Two things in particular come to mind; the first one was at Ascot Racecourse. In the old days, late sixties in particular, the racecourse put on a show simply called "The Ascot Jumping Show" and many of the top riders came to compete.

ᙍ

I walked down to the collecting ring one day and saw this jolly lady in jeans and a sweater and we started a wonderful conversation, getting on like a house on fire. We laughed and shared things about the show jumping world and she introduced herself to me as Sarah. I found out later that day that it was Lady Sarah Fitzalan-Howard, the daughter of the Duke and Duchess of Norfolk. Sarah had represented Great Britain with a horse called Orskeit and during our conversation; I had no idea that she was related to her Majesty the Queen. I liked Sarah a lot and for the rest of the show at Ascot she and I were friends. I actually felt sad when I had to go back up north and say goodbye to my new best friend.

One of the luxuries of Ascot was the management opened up the bathing facilities for us, the ones used by the Jockey's during race meeting and low and behold we had bathrooms with full baths to actually bath and wash in.

You can imagine the lines of riders and grooms who were desperate to get in to these prized bath rooms to just lay back and soak in some wonderful hot water and wash ourselves in full luxury. I remember beating David Bowen into one of the bathrooms, I stripped off and jumped into this wonderful deep tub and he banged like crazy on the door and threatened to break it down. I was shocked, because knowing David at that time; I thought he was being serious. It was all good clean fun.

CB

My next memory of this happening was at Wembley, the first time the British Show Jumping Association held the Royal International Horse show at Wembley Stadium. Owing to traffic congestion and it becoming unsafe, we could no longer bring horses to the White City. So, we ended up with a new home and actually jumping our horses on the hallowed turf of the most prized football stadium in the world.

To us Show Jumpers, the biggest thrill was once again management of Wembley Stadium opening up the bathing facilities for us once again. Of course, these were the enormous baths that had been used for many years by some of the most famous footballers of all time. I did not really care about that because right there in the middle of the players bathing room was an enormous bathtub that held about twenty people. I can remember Simon Rogerson from Scotland and David Broome filling it with the most wonderful hot water. Apart from them, there was myself, John Bailey, Andrew Fielder, Graham Fletcher, David Boston Barker and several others waiting to try it out. We all dived in and the water immediately splashed like crazy over the sides and flooded the floor. I do remember however, the floor was tiled and had drains every few feet so we did not end up getting in trouble for flooding out the footballers dressing rooms.

We did get in trouble for something else though, after the second year of holding the Royal International Horse Show at Wembley

Stadium, the F.A.A. said, "Enough is enough" and banned us from ever jumping our horses again on the prized turf of Wembley Stadium.

It was understandable really as the constant jumping, the rain and wear and tear on the pitch caused a lot of damage and it cost thousands to put it right. This meant once again that the Royal International had to find a new home.

Another venue was found, and the following year we moved across the way to the Empire Pool, the home of the Horse of the Year Show. It was not the same having it there because being indoors; it sort of had the same atmosphere as the Horse of the Year Show, which was held in October. We did not mind that, however, many thought that as it was July, we should be competing as tradition had always been for the R.I.H.S. in an outdoor venue.

Eventually a permanent outdoor home once again was found, not in London, but down at Hickstead in Sussex which is now the home to the Royal International Horse Show.

Frank Waters

I do hope you will join me for Volume 2 of The Golden Age of Show Jumping. We've an endless catalogue of wonderful horses and riders to celebrate, honor and to share with you all. I have been asked to pick up my story where I left off here in Volume 1. I think I may have some writing to do. Until next time my friends.

Printed in Great Britain
by Amazon

14961170R00122